The Constitution of
The State of Missouri:
A Quick Reference Guide

Bootblack Budget Books
Copyright 2018 ©
ISBN-13: 978-1986826433
ISBN-10: 1986826430

Contents

Preamble – Page 37

Article I: Bill of Rights – Page 38

Section 1. Source of Political Power—Origin, Basis and Aim of Government

Section 2. Promotion of General Welfare—Natural Rights of Persons—Equality Under the Law—Purpose of Government

Section 3. Powers of the People Over Internal Affairs, Constitution and Form of Government

Section 4. Independence of Missouri—Submission of Certain Amendments to Constitution of the United States

Section 5. Religious Freedom—Liberty of Conscience and Belief—Limitations—Right to Pray—Academic Religious Freedoms and Prayer

Section 6. Practice and Support of Religion Not Compulsory—Contracts Therefor Enforceable

Section 7. Public Aid for Religious Purposes—Preferences and Discriminations On Religious Grounds

Section 8. Freedom of Speech—Evidence of Truth in Defamation Actions—Province of Jury

Section 9. Rights of Peaceable Assembly and Petition

Section 10. Due Process of Law

Section 11. Imprisonment for Debt

Section 12. Habeas Corpus

Section 13. Ex Post Facto Laws—Impairment of Contracts—Irrevocable Privileges

Section 14. Open Courts—Certain Remedies—Justice Without Sale, Denial Or Delay

Section 15. Unreasonable Search and Seizure Prohibited—Contents and Basis of Warrants

Section 16. Grand Juries—Composition—Jurisdiction to Convene—Powers

Section 17. Indictments and Informations in Criminal Cases—Exceptions

Section 18(A). Rights of Accused in Criminal Prosecutions

Section 18(B). Depositions in Felony Cases

Section 18(C). Admissibility of Evidence

Section 19. Self-Incrimination and Double Jeopardy

Section 20. Bail Guaranteed—Exceptions

Section 21. Excessive Bail and Fines—Cruel and Unusual Punishment

Section 22(A). Right of Trial by Jury—Qualification of Jurors—Two-Thirds Verdict

Section 22(B). Female Jurors—Optional Exemption

Section 23. Right to Keep and Bear Arms, Ammunition, and Certain Accessories—Exception—Rights to be Unalienable

Section 24. Subordination of Military to Civil Power—Quartering Soldiers

Section 25. Elections and Right of Suffrage

Section 26. Compensation for Property Taken by Eminent Domain—Condemnation Juries—Payment—Railroad Property

Section 27. Acquisition of Excess Property by Eminent Domain—Disposition Under Restrictions

Section 28. Limitation On Taking of Private Property for Private Use—Exceptions—Public Use A Judicial Question

Section 29. Organized Labor and Collective Bargaining

Section 30. Treason—Attainder—Corruption of Blood and Forfeitures—Estate of Suicides—Death by Casualty

Section 31. Fines Or Imprisonments Fixed by Administrative Agencies

Section 32. Crime Victims Rights

Section 33. Marriage, Validity and Recognition

Section 34. English to be the Official Language in This State

Section 35. Right to Farm

Article II: The Distribution of Powers – Page 51

Section 1. Three Departments of Government—Separation of Powers

Article III: Legislative Department – Page 52

Section 1. Legislative Power—General Assembly

Section 2. Election of Representatives—Apportionment Commission, Appointment, Duties, Compensation

Section 3. Repealed

Section 4. Qualifications of Representatives

Section 5. Senators—Number—Senatorial Districts

Section 6. Qualifications of Senators

Section 7. Senatorial Apportionment Commission—Number, Appointment, Duties, Compensation

Section 8. Term Limitations for Members of General Assembly

Section 9. Apportionment of Representatives

Section 10. Basis of Apportionment—Alteration of Districts

Section 11. Time of Election of Senators and Representatives

Section 12. Members of General Assembly Disqualified From Holding Other Offices

Section 13. Vacation of Office by Removal of Residence

Section 14. Writs of Election to Fill Vacancies

Section 15. Oath of Office of Members of Assembly—Administration—Effect of Refusal to Take Oath and Conviction of Violation

Section 16. Compensation, Mileage Allowance and Expenses of General Assembly Members

Section 17. Limitation On Number of Legislative Employees

Section 18. Appointment of Officers of Houses—Jurisdiction to Determine Membership—Power to Make Rules, Punish for Contempt and Disorderly Conduct and Expel Members

Section 19. Legislative Privileges

Section 20. Regular Sessions of Assembly—Quorum—Compulsory Attendance—Public Sessions—Limitation On Power to Adjourn

Section 20(A). Automatic Adjournment—Tabling of Bills, When

Section 20(B). Special Session, Procedure to Convene—Limitations—Automatic Adjournment

Legislative Proceedings – Page 63

Section 21. Style of Laws—Bills—Limitation On Amendments—Power of Each House to Originate and Amend Bills—Reading of Bills

Section 22. Referral of Bills to Committees—Recall of Referred Bills—Records of Committees—Provision for Interim Meetings

Section 23. Limitation of Scope of Bills—Contents of Titles—Exceptions

Section 24. Printing of Bills and Amendments

Section 25. Limitation On Introduction of Bills

Section 26. Legislative Journals—Demand for Yeas and Nays—Manner and Record of Vote

Section 27. Concurrence in Amendments—Adoption of Conference Committee Reports—Final Passage of Bills

Section 28. Form of Reviving, Reenacting and Amending Bills

Section 29. Effective Date of Laws—Exceptions—Procedure in Emergencies and Upon Recess

Section 30. Signing of Bills by Presiding Officers—Procedure On Objections—Presentation of Bills to Governor

Section 31. Governor's Duty As to Bills and Joint Resolutions—Time Limitations—Failure to Return, Bill Becomes Law

Section 32. Vetoed Bills Reconsidered, When

Section 33. Repealed

Section 34. Revision of General Statutes—Limitation On Compensation

Section 35. Committee On Legislative Research

Limitation of Legislative Power – Page 68

Section 36. Payment of State Revenues and Receipts to Treasury—Limitation of Withdrawals to Appropriations—Order of Appropriations

Section 37. Limitation On State Debts and Bond Issues

Section 37(A). State Building Bond Issue Authorized—Interest Rate—Payment From Income Tax and Other Funds

Section 37(B). Water Pollution Control Fund Established—Bonds Authorized—Funds to Stand Appropriated

Section 37(C). Additional Water Pollution Control Bonds Authorized—Procedure

Section 37(D). Third State Building Bond Issue Authorized—Procedures—Use of Funds

Section 37(E). Water Pollution Control, Improvement of Drinking Water Systems and Storm Water Control—Bonds Authorized, Procedure

Section 37(F). Fourth State Building Bond and Interest Fund Created—Bond Issue Authorized, Procedure—Use of Funds

Section 37(G). Rural Water and Sewer Grants and Loans—Bonds Authorized, Procedure

Section 37(H). Stormwater Control—Bonds Authorized, Procedure

Section 38(A). Limitation On Use of State Funds and Credit—Exceptions—Public Calamity—Blind Pensions—Old Age Assistance—Aid to Children—Direct Relief—Adjusted Compensation for Veterans—Rehabilitation—Participation in Federal Aid

Section 38(B). Tax Levy for Blind Pension Fund

Section 38(C). Neighborhood Improvement Districts, Cities and Counties May be Authorized to Establish, Powers and Duties—Limitation On Indebtedness

Section 38(D). Stem Cell Research—Title of Law—Permissible Research—Violations, Penalty—Report Required, When—Prohibited Acts—Definitions

Section 39. Limitation of Power of General Assembly

Section 39(A). Bingo May be Authorized—Requirements

State Lottery – Page 108

Section 39(B). State Lottery, Authority to Establish—Lottery Proceeds Fund Established, Purpose

Section 39(C). Pari-Mutuel Wagering May be Authorized by General Assembly—Horse Racing Commission Established, Election Procedure to Adopt Or Reject Horse Racing

Section 39(D). Gaming Revenues to be Appropriated to Public Institutions of Elementary, Secondary and Higher Education

Section 39(E). Riverboat Gambling Authorized On Missouri and Mississippi Rivers—Boats in Moats Authorized

Section 39(F). Raffles and Sweepstakes Authorized

Section 40. Limitations On Passage of Local and Special Laws

Section 41. Indirect Enactment of Local and Special Laws—Repeal of Local and Special Laws

Section 42. Notice of Proposed Local Or Special Laws

Section 43. Title and Control of Lands of United States—Exemption From Taxation—Taxation of Lands of Nonresidents

Section 44. Uniform Interest Rates

Section 45. Congressional Apportionment

Section 45(A). Term Limitations for Members of U.S. Congress—Effective When—Voluntary Observance Required, When

Section 46. Militia

Section 46(A). Emergency Duties and Powers of Assembly On Enemy Attack

Section 47. State Parks—Appropriations for, Required

Section 48. Historical Memorials and Monuments—Acquisition of Property

Initiative and Referendum – Page 119

Section 49. Reservation of Power to Enact and Reject Laws

Section 50. Initiative Petitions—Signatures Required—Form and Procedure

Section 51. Appropriations by Initiative—Effective Date of Initiated Laws—Conflicting Laws Concurrently Adopted

Section 52(A). Referendum—Exceptions—Procedure

Section 52(B). Veto Power—Elections—Effective Date

Section 53. Basis for Computation of Signatures Required

Article IV: Executive Department – Page 122

Section 1. Executive Power—The Governor

Section 2. Duties of Governor

Section 3. Qualifications of Governor

Section 4. Power of Appointment to Fill Vacancies—Tenure of Appointees

Section 5. Commissions of State Officers

Section 6. Commander in Chief of Militia—Authority

Section 7. Reprieves, Commutations and Pardons—Limitations On Power

Section 8. Concurrent Resolutions—Duty of Governor—Exceptions—Limitation of Effect

Section 9. Governor's Messages and Recommendations to Assembly—Call of Extra Sessions

Section 10. Lieutenant Governor—Qualifications, Powers and Duties

Section 11(A). Order of Succession to Governorship, When

Section 11(B). Governor's Declaration of Disability, Effect of—Disability Board, Membership, Duties—Governor to Resume Office, When—Disputed Illness, Supreme Court to Decide

Section 11(C). Acting As Governor Not to Vacate Regular Office

Section 12. Executive Department, Composition of—Elective Officials—Departments and Offices Enumerated

Section 13. State Auditor—Qualifications and Duties—Limitations On Duties

Section 14. Secretary of State—Duties—State Seal—Official Register—Limitation On Duties

Section 15. State Treasurer—Duties—Custody, Investment and Deposit of State Funds—Duties Limited—Nonstate Funds to be in Custody and Invested by Department of Revenue—Nonstate Funds Defined

Section 16. Filing of Administrative Rules and Regulations

Section 17. Elective State Officers—Time of Election and Terms—Limitation On Reelection—Selection of Department Heads—Removal and Qualifications of Appointive Officers

Section 18. Election Returns—Board of State Canvassers—Time of Meeting and Duties—Requirement for Election—Tie Votes

Section 19. Department Personnel—Selection and Removal—Merit System—Veterans' Preference

Section 20. Location of Executive and Administrative Offices

Section 21. Limitation On Changes of Salaries—Fees, Costs

Revenue – Page 132

Section 22. Department of Revenue, Duties of—Director, Appointment of

Section 23. Fiscal Year—Limitations On Appropriations—Specification of Amount and Purpose

Section 24. Governor's Budget and Recommendations As to Revenue—Proposed Legislation Not Enacted Not to be Included in Projection of New Revenues

Section 25. Limitation of Governor's Budget On Power of Appropriations

Section 26. Power of Partial Veto of Appropriation Bills—Procedure—Limitations

Section 27. Power of Governor to Control Rate of and Reduce Expenditures—Notification General Assembly, When

Section 27(A). Cash Operating Reserve Fund Established—Investment—Excess Transfer to General Revenue, When

Section 27(B). Facilities Maintenance and Review Fund Created, Purpose—State Facilities, Defined—Transfer of Monies Into Fund, Reduction Or Elimination of Transfer by Governor

Section 28. Treasury Withdrawals, How Made, Certified How—Appropriation, Period of

Highways and Transportation – Page 139

Section 29. Highways and Transportation Commission—Qualifications of Members and Employees—Authority Over State Highways and Other Transportation Programs

Section 30(A). Apportionment of Motor Vehicle Fuel Tax—Limitation On Local Fuel Taxes

Section 30(B). Source and Application of State Road Fund and State Transportation Fund

Section 30(C). Transportation Programs and Facilities, Administration of by Commission

Section 31. State Highways in Municipalities

Section 32. Apportionment of Funds for Supplementary State Highways

Section 32(A). Repealed

Section 33. Retirement Benefits Not Changed

Section 34. Recognition of Outstanding Bonds—Determination, Certification and Collection of Annual State Highway Bond Tax

Agriculture – Page 152

Section 35. Agriculture, Department of—Director, How Appointed—Funds to be Provided, How

Section 36. Forestry and Forest Fires

Economic Development – Page 152

Section 36(A). Economic Development, Department of—Duties of Department—Director, How Appointed

Insurance – Page 153

Section 36(B). Department of Insurance, Established—Director, Appointment—Office of Consumer Affairs to be Established Within Department, Duties

Social Services – Page 153

Section 37. Social Services, Department of—Duties of Department—Director, How Appointed

Mental Health – Page 153

Section 37(A). Mental Health, Department of—Duties of Department—Director, How Appointed

Section 38. Repealed

Section 39. Cooperation With Federal and Other State Governments

Conservation – Page 154

Section 40(A). Conservation Commission, Members, Qualifications, Terms, How Appointed—Duties of Commission—Expenses of Members

Section 40(B). Incumbent Members

Section 41. Acquisition of Property—Eminent Domain

Section 42. Director of Conservation and Personnel of Commission

Section 43(A). Sales Tax, Use for Conservation Purposes

Section 43(B). Use of Revenue and Funds of Conservation Commission

Section 43(C). Effective Date—Self-Enforcability

Section 44. Self-Enforcability—Enabling Clause—Repealing Clause

Section 45. Rules and Regulations—Filing—Review

Section 46. Distribution of Rules and Regulations

Natural Resources – Page 158

Section 47. Natural Resources, Department of—Duties of Department—Director, How Appointed

Section 47(A). Sales and Use Tax Levied for Soil and Water Conservation and for State Parks—Distribution of Parks Sales Tax Fund to Counties, Purpose, Limitation

Section 47(B). Disbursement of Revenue, Purposes

Section 47(C). Provisions Self-Enforcing, Exception—Not Part of General Revenue Or Expense of State—Effective and Expiration Dates

Public Safety – Page 160

Section 48. Public Safety, Department of—Duties of Department —Director, How Appointed

Labor and Industrial Relations – Page 160

Section 49. Labor and Industrial Relations, Department of— Duties—Commission Members, How Appointed, Terms, Qualifications

Office of Administration – Page 161

Section 50. Administration, Office of—Commissioner, How Appointed

Appointment of Administrative Heads – Page 161

Section 51. Appointments, How Made—Failure to Confirm, Effect of

Higher Education – Page 162

Section 52. Higher Education, Department of Established— Coordinating Board for Higher Education Established, Members, Terms, Qualifications

Nondiscrimination in Appointments – Page 162

Section 53. Discrimination As to Race, Creed, Color Or National Origin Prohibited

Article V: Judicial Department – Page 163

Section 1. Judicial Power—Constitutional Courts

Section 2. Supreme Court—Controlling Decisions—Number of Judges—Sessions

Section 3. Jurisdiction of the Supreme Court

Section 4. Superior Courts to Control Inferior Courts—Courts Administrator, Salary—Reapportionment Commission, Appointment

Section 5. Rules of Practice and Procedure—Duty of Supreme Court—Power of Legislature

Section 6. Assignment of Judges—Authority of Supreme Court—Eligible Judges

Section 7. Supreme Court and Court of Appeals May Sit in Divisions

Section 8. Chief Justice and Chief Judges, Election, Terms—Authority of Chief Justice

Section 9. Transfer of Causes to Supreme Court En Banc

Section 10. Transfer of Cases From Court of Appeals to Supreme Court—Scope of Review

Section 11. Want of Jurisdiction, Effect—Transfers

Section 12. Judicial Opinions—Filing and Publication—Memorandum Decisions and Orders

Section 13. Court of Appeals, Districts, Judges

Section 14. Circuit Courts—Jurisdiction—Sessions

Section 15. Judicial Circuits—Establishment and Changes—General Terms and Divisions—Judges—Presiding Judge—Court Personnel

Section 16. Associate Circuit Judges, Selection

Section 17. Associate Circuit Judges, Jurisdiction

Section 18. Judicial Review of Action of Administrative Agencies—Scope of Review

Section 19. Terms of Judges

Section 20. Salaries and Compensation of Judges—Provision Against Other Special Compensation and Practice of Law—Travel and Other Expenses

Section 21. Judges—Qualifications—Age Requirements—License to Practice Law

Section 22. Court of Appeals Clerks and Personnel—Salaries

Section 23. Municipal Judges and Court Personnel—Selection—Terms—Compensation—Jurisdiction—Appeals—Role of Associate Circuit Judges

Section 24. Retirement, Removal and Discipline of Judges, Commission On—Composition, Terms, Duties, Procedures, Reimbursement of Expenses—Additional Duties Prohibited

Section 25(A). Nonpartisan Selection of Judges—Courts Subject to Plan—Appointments to Fill Vacancies

Section 25(B). Adoption of Plan in Other Circuits—Petitions and Elections—Form of Petition Ballots

Section 25(C) (1). Tenure of Judges—Declaration of Candidacy—Form of Judicial Ballot—Rejection and Retention

Section 25(C) (2). Certification of Names Upon Declaration—Law Applicable to Elections

Section 25(D). Nonpartisan Judicial Commissions—Number, Qualifications, Selection and Terms of Members—Majority Rule—Reimbursement of Expenses—Rules of Supreme Court

Section 25(E). Payment of Expenses

Section 25(F). Prohibition of Political Activity by Judges

Section 25(G). Self-Enforceability

Section 26. Retirement—Assignment As Senior Judge Or Commissioner

Schedule – Page 180

Section 27. Effective Date and Transition Provisions

21

Article VI: Local Government – Page 191

Section 1. Recognition of Existing Counties

Section 2. Continuation of Existing Organization of Counties

Section 3. Consolidation of Counties—Allocation of Liabilities

Section 4. Division Or Diminution of Counties

Section 5. Dissolution of Counties—Annexation

Section 6. Removal of County Seats

Section 7. County Courts—Number of Members—Powers and Duties

Section 8. Classification of Counties—Revisions to Article Vi Passed by The 88th General Assembly to be Retroactive

Section 9. Alternative Forms of County Government.

Section 10. Terms of City and County Offices

Section 11. Compensation of County Officers—Increases in Compensation Not to Require Additional Services—State Ment of Fees and Salaries

Section 12. Officers Compensated Only by Salaries in Certain Counties

Section 13. Compensation of Officers in Criminal Matters—Fees

Section 14. Joint Participation by Counties in Common Enterprises

Section 15. Classification of Cities and Towns—Uniform Laws—Change From Special to General Law

Section 16. Cooperation by Local Governments With Other Governmental Units

Section 17. Consolidation and Separation As Between Municipalities and Other Political Subdivisions

Special Charters – Page 196

Section 18(A). County Government by Special Charter—Limitations—Counties Adopting Charter Or Constitutional Form Shall be A Separate Class of Counties From Classification System

Section 18(B). Provisions Required in County Charters—Exception

Section 18(C). Provisions Authorized in County Charters—Participation by County in Government of Other Local Units

Section 18(D). Taxation Under County Charters

Section 18(E). Laws Affecting Charter Counties—Limitations

Section 18(F). Petitions for Charter Commissions—Signatures Required—Procedure

Section 18(G). Charter Commission—Appointment, Number and Qualification of Members

Section 18(H). Adoption of Charter—Special Election—Manner of Submission

Section 18(I). Notice of Special Charter Election

Section 18(J). Certificates of Adoption of Charter—Recordation and Deposit—Judicial Notice

Section 18(K). Amendments of County Charters

Section 18(L). Limitation On Resubmission After Defeat of Charter

Section 18(M). County of the First Classification May Provide A County Constitution—Content, Procedure, Limitations

Section 18(N). Circuit Judges May Appoint Constitution Commission, Members, Qualifications

Section 18(O). County Constitution Effective When—Submission to Electorate for Separate Vote On Any Part Or Alternative Sections

Section 18(P). Publication Requirements for Text of Constitution—Election to Adopt Procedure

Section 18(Q). Constitution May be Adopted Or Rejected by Voters—Resubmission Procedure

Section 18(R). Certified Copies of County Constitution to be Filed, Where—Amendments to Constitution, Procedure

Local Government – Page 202

Section 19. Certain Cities May Adopt Charter Form of Government—Procedure to Frame and Adopt—Notice Required—Effect of

Section 19(A). Power of Charter Cities, How Limited

Section 20. Amendment to City Charters—Procedure to Submit and Adopt

Section 21. Reclamation of Blighted, Substandard Or Insanitary Areas

Section 22. Laws Affecting Charter Cities—Officers and Employees

Finances – Page 205

Section 23. Limitation On Ownership of Corporate Stock, Use of Credit and Grants of Public Funds by Local Governments

Section 23(A). Cities May Acquire and Furnish Industrial Plants —Indebtedness for

Section 24. Annual Budgets and Reports of Local Government and Municipally Owned Utilities—Audits

Section 25. Limitation On Use of Credit and Grant of Public Funds by Local Governments—Pensions and Retirement Plans for Employees of Certain Cities and Counties

Section 26(A). Limitation On Indebtedness of Local Governments Without Popular Vote

Section 26(B). Limitation On Indebtedness of Local Government Authorized by Popular Vote

Section 26(C). Additional Indebtedness of Counties and Cities When Authorized by Popular Vote

Section 26(D). Additional Indebtedness of Cities for Public Improvements—Benefit Districts—Special Assessments

Section 26(E). Additional Indebtedness of Cities for Municipally Owned Water and Light Plants—Limitations

Section 26(F). Annual Tax to Pay and Retire Obligations Within Twenty Years

Section 26(G). Contest of Elections to Authorize Indebtedness. 27. Political Subdivision Revenue Bonds for Utility, Industrial and Airport Purposes—Restrictions

Local Government – Page 210

Section 27(A). Political Subdivision Revenue Bonds Issued for Utilities and Airports, Restrictions

Section 27(B). Political Subdivision Revenue Bonds Issued for Industrial Development, Restriction

Section 27(C). Revenue Bonds Defined

Section 28. Refunding Bonds

Section 29. Application of Funds Derived From Public Debt

City and County of St. Louis – Page 212

Section 30(A). Powers Conferred With Respect to Intergovernmental Relations—Procedure for Selection of Board of Free-Holders

Section 30(B). Appointment of Member by Governor—Meetings of Board—Vacancies—Compensation and Reimbursement of Members—Preparation of Plan—Taxation of Real Estate Affected —Submission At Special Elections—Effect of Adoption— Certification and Recordation—Judicial Notice

City of St. Louis – Page 216

Section 31. Recognition of City of St. Louis As Now Existing Both As A City and A County

Section 32(A). Amendment of Charter of St. Louis

Section 32(B). Revision of Charter of St. Louis—Officers to Complete Terms and Staff Given Opportunity for City Employment

Section 32(C). Effect of Revision On Retirement

Section 33. Certification, Recordation and Deposit of Amendments and Revised Charter—Judicial Notice

Article VII: Public Officers – Page 218

Section 1. Impeachment—Officers Liable—Grounds

Section 2. Power of Impeachment—Trial of Impeachments

Section 3. Effect of Judgment of Impeachment

Section 4. Removal of Officers Not Subject to Impeachment

Section 5. Election Contests—Executive State Officers—Other Election Contests

Section 6. Penalty for Nepotism

Section 7. Appointment of Officers

Section 8. Qualifications for Public Office—Nonresidents

Section 9. Disqualification by Federal Employment—Exceptions

Section 10. Equality of Sexes in Public Service

Section 11. Oath of Office

Section 12. Tenure of Office

Section 13. Limitation On Increase of Compensation and Extension of Terms of Office

Section 14. Statement of Actuary Required Before Retirement Benefits Substantially Change

Article VIII: Suffrage and Elections – Page 222

Section 1. Time of General Elections

Section 2. Qualifications of Voters—Disqualifications

Section 3. Methods of Voting—Secrecy of Ballot—Exceptions

Section 4. Privilege of Voters From Arrest—Exceptions

Section 5. Registration of Voters

Section 6. Retention of Residence for Voting Purposes

Section 7. Absentee Voting

Section 15. Preamble

Section 16. Congressional Term Limits Amendment

Section 17. Voter Instruction On Term Limits for Members of Congress—Ballots to Include "disregarded Voters' Instruction On Term Limits", When

Section 18. Voter Instruction On Term Limit Pledge for Non-Incumbents

Section 19. Secretary of State, Duties Regarding Ballot Designations

Section 20. Automatic Repeal

Section 21. Legal Challenges, Jurisdiction

Section 22. Severability

Article IX: Education – Page 230

Section 1(A). Free Public Schools—Age Limit

Section 1(B). Specific Schools—Adult Education

Section 2(A). State Board of Education—Number and Appointment of Members—Political Affiliation—Terms—Reimbursement and Compensation

Section 2(B). Commissioner of Education—Qualification, Duties and Compensation—Appointment and Compensation of Professional Staff—Powers and Duties of State Board of Education

Section 3(A). Payment and Distribution of Appropriations and Income

Section 3(B). Deficiency in Provision for Eight-Month School Year—Allotment of State Revenue for School Purposes

Section 3(C). Racial Discrimination in Employment of Teachers

Section 4. Public School and Seminary Funds—Certificates of Indebtedness—Renewals—Liquidation—Legal Investment of Funds—Tax Levy for Interest

Section 5. Public School Fund—Sources—Payment Into State Treasury—Investment—Limitation On Use of Income

Section 6. Seminary Fund—Sources—Payment Into State Treasury—Investment—Limitation On Use of Income

Section 7. County and Township School Funds—Liquidation and Reinvestment—Optional Distribution On Liquidation—Annual Distribution of Income and Receipts

Section 8. Prohibition of Public Aid for Religious Purposes and Institutions

Section 9(A). State University—Government by Board of Curators—Number and Appointment

Section 9(B). Maintenance of State University and Other Educational Institutions

Section 10. Free Public Libraries—Declaration of Policy—State Aid to Local Public Libraries

Article X: Taxation – Page 236

Section 1. Taxing Power—Exercise by State and Local Governments

Section 2. Inalienability of Power to Tax

Section 3. Limitation of Taxation to Public Purposes—Uniformity—General Laws—Time for Payment of Taxes—Valuation

Section 4(A). Classification of Taxable Property—Taxes On Franchises, Incomes, Excises and Licenses

Section 4(B). Basis of Assessment of Tangible Property—Real Property—Taxation of Intangibles—Limitations

Section 4(C). Assessment, Levy, Collection and Distribution of Tax On Intangibles

Section 4(D). Income Tax Laws, May Incorporate Federal Laws by Reference—Rates, How Set

Section 5. Taxation of Railroads

Section 6. Property Exempt From Taxation

Section 6(A). Homestead Exemption Authorized

Section 6(B). Intangible Property Exempt From Taxation, When—Local Governments May be Reimbursed, When

Section 7. Relief From Taxation—Forest Lands—Obsolete, Decadent, Or Blighted Areas—Limitations—Exception

Section 8. Limitation On State Tax Rate On Tangible Property

Section 9. Immunity of Private Property From Sale for Municipal Debts

Section 10(A). Exclusion of State From Local Taxation for Local Purposes

Section 10(B). State Aid for Local Purposes

Section 10(C). Reduction in Rates of Levy May be Required by Law

Section 11(A). Taxing Jurisdiction of Local Governments—Limitation On Assessed Valuation

Section 11(B). Limitations On Local Tax Rates

Section 11(C). Increase of Tax Rate by Popular Vote—Further Limitation by Law—Exceptions to Limitation

Section 11(D). Tax Rate in St. Louis for County Purposes

Section 11(E). Exclusion of Bonded Debt From Limitations On Tax Rates

Section 11(F). Authorization of Local Taxes Other Than Ad Valorem Taxes

Section 11(G). Operating Levy for Kansas City School Districts May be Set by School Board

Section 12(A). Additional Tax Rates for County Roads and Bridges—Road Districts—Reduction in Rate May be Required, How

Section 12(B). Refund of Road and Bridge Taxes

Section 13. Tax Sales—Limitations—Contents of Notices

Section 14. Equalization Commission—Appointment—Duties

Section 15. Definition of "other Political Subdivision

Section 16. Taxes and State Spending to be Limited—State to Support Certain Local Activities—Emergency Spending and Bond Payments to be Authorized

Section 17. Definitions

Section 18. Limitation On Taxes Which May be Imposed by General Assembly—Exclusions—Refund of Excess Revenue—Adjustments Authorized

Section 18(E) Voter Approval Required for Taxes Or Fees, When, Exceptions—Definitions—Compliance Procedure, Remedies

Section 19. Limits May be Exceeded, When, How

Section 20. Limitation On State Expenses

Section 21. State Support to Local Governments Not to be Reduced, Additional Activities and Services Not to be Imposed Without Full State Funding

Section 22. Political Subdivisions to Receive Voter Approval for Increases in Taxes and Fees—Rollbacks May be Required—Limitation Not Applicable to Taxes for Bonds

Section 23. Taxpayers May Bring Actions for Interpretations of Limitations

Section 24. Voter Approval Requirements Not Exclusive—Self-Enforceability

Section 25. Sale Or Transfer of Homes Or Other Real Estate, Prohibition On Imposition of Any New Taxes, When

Article XI: Corporations – Page 255

Section 1. Definition of "corporation"

Section 2. Organization of Corporations by General Law—Special Laws Relating to Corporations—Invalidation of Unexercised Charters and Franchises

Section 3. Exercise of Police Power With Respect to Corporations

Section 4. Corporations Subject to Eminent Domain—Trial by Jury

Section 5. Repealed

Section 6. Cumulative Voting Authorized Unless Alternate Method Provided by Law—Exceptions

Section 7. Consideration for Corporate Stock and Debts—Fictitious Issues—Antecedent Debts—Increases of Stock Or Bonds— Issuance of Preferred Stock

Section 8. Limitation of Liability of Stockholders

Railroads – Page 257

Section 9. Public Highways—Common Carriers—Regulations

Section 10. Consolidation of Domestic With Foreign Railroad Corporations—Jurisdiction of Missouri Courts—Notice of Consolidation

Section 11. Local Consent for Street Railroads

Section 12. Prohibition of Discrimination, Favoritism and Preferences

Banks – Page 258

Section 13. Exclusion of State From Banking

Article XII: Amending the Constitution – Page 259

Section 1. Limitation On Revision and Amendment

Section 2(A). Proposal of Amendments by General Assembly

Section 2(B). Submission of Amendments Proposed by General Assembly Or by the Initiative

Section 3(A). Referendum On Constitutional Convention—Qualifications of Delegates—Selection of Nominees for District Delegates and Delegates-At-Large—Election Procedure

Section 3(B). Convention of Delegates—Quarters—Oath—Compensation—Quorum—Vote Required—Organization, Employees, Printing—Public Sessions—Rules—Vacancies

Section 3(C). Submission of Proposal Adopted by Convention—Time of Election—Effective Date

Schedule – Page 262

Section 1. Supersession of Prior Constitutional Provisions

Section 2. Effect On Existing Laws

Section 3. Effect On Existing Terms of Office

Section 4. Effect On Certain Existing Courts

Section 5. Effect On Existing Rights, Claims

Section 6. Reimbursement for Expenses of Constitutional Election

Article XIII: Public Employees – Page 264

Section 1. Medical Benefits May be Authorized for State Officers, Employees and Their Dependents

Section 2. Medical Benefits May be Authorized for Political Subdivision Officers, Employees and Their Dependents

Section 3. Compensation of State Elected Officials, General Assembly Members and Judges to be Set by Missouri Citizens Commission On Compensation—Members Qualifications, Terms, Removal, Vacancies, Duties—Procedure

PREAMBLE:

We, the people of Missouri, with profound reverence for the Supreme Ruler of the Universe, and grateful for His goodness, do establish this Constitution for the better government of the state.

ARTICLE I: BILL OF RIGHTS

Section 1. Source of Political Power—Origin, Basis and Aim of Government

That all political power is vested in and derived from the people; that all government of right originates from the people, is founded upon their will only, and is instituted solely for the good of the whole.

Section 2. Promotion of General Welfare—Natural Rights of Persons—Equality Under the Law—Purpose of Government

That all constitutional government is intended to promote the general welfare of the people; that all persons have a natural right to life, liberty, the pursuit of happiness and the enjoyment of the gains of their own industry; that all persons are created equal and are entitled to equal rights and opportunity under the law; that to give security to these things is the principal office of government, and that when government does not confer this security, it fails in its chief design.

Section 3. Powers of the People Over Internal Affairs, Constitution and Form of Government

That the people of this state have the inherent, sole and exclusive right to regulate the internal government and police thereof, and to alter and abolish their constitution and form of government whenever they may deem it necessary to their safety and happiness, provided such change be not repugnant to the Constitution of the United States.

Section 4. Independence of Missouri—Submission of Certain Amendments to Constitution of the United States

That Missouri is a free and independent state, subject only to the Constitution of the United States; that all proposed amendments to the Constitution of the United States qualifying or affecting the individual liberties of the people or which in any wise may impair the right of local self-government belonging to the people of this state, should be submitted to conventions of the people.

Section 5. Religious Freedom—Liberty of Conscience and Belief—Limitations— Right to Pray—Academic Religious Freedoms and Prayer

That all men and women have a natural and indefeasible right to worship Almighty God according to the dictates of their own consciences; that no human authority can control or interfere with the rights of conscience; that no person shall, on account of his or her religious persuasion or belief, be rendered ineligible to any public office or trust or profit in this state, be disqualified from testifying or serving as a juror, or be molested in his or her person or estate; that to secure a citizen's right to acknowledge Almighty God according to the dictates of his or her own conscience, neither the state nor any of its political subdivisions shall establish any official religion, nor shall a citizen's right to pray or express his or her religious beliefs be infringed; that the state shall not coerce any person to participate in any prayer or other religious activity, but shall ensure that any person shall have the right to pray individually or corporately in a private or public setting so long as such prayer does not result in disturbance of the peace or disruption of a public meeting or assembly; that citizens as well as elected officials and employees of the state of Missouri and its political subdivisions shall have the right to pray on government premises and public property so long as such prayers abide within the same parameters placed upon any other free speech under similar circumstances; that the General Assembly and the governing bodies of political subdivisions may extend to ministers, clergy-persons, and other individuals the privilege to offer invocations or other prayers at meetings or sessions of the General Assembly or governing bodies; that students may express their beliefs about religion in written and oral assignments free from discrimination based on the religious content of their work; that no student shall be compelled to perform or participate in academic assignments or educational presentations that violate his or her religious beliefs; that the state shall ensure public school students their right to free exercise of religious expression without interference, as long as such prayer or other expression is private and voluntary, whether individually or corporately, and in a manner that is not disruptive and as long as such prayers or expressions abide within the same parameters placed upon any other free speech under similar circumstances; and, to emphasize the right to free exercise of religious expression, that all free public schools receiving state appropriations shall display, in a conspicuous and legible manner, the text of the Bill of Rights of the Constitution of the United States; but this section shall not be construed to expand the rights of prisoners in state or local custody beyond those afforded by the laws of the United States, excuse acts of licentiousness, nor to justify practices inconsistent with the good order, peace or safety of the state, or with the rights of others.

Section 6. Practice and Support of Religion Not Compulsory—Contracts Therefor Enforceable

That no person can be compelled to erect, support or attend any place or system of worship, or to maintain or support any priest, minister, preacher or teacher of any sect, church, creed or denomination of religion; but if any person shall voluntarily make a contract for any such object, he shall be held to the performance of the same.

Section 7. Public Aid for Religious Purposes—Preferences and Discriminations On Religious Grounds

That no money shall ever be taken from the pub lic treasury, directly or indirectly, in aid of any church, sect or denomination of religion, or in aid of any priest, preacher, minister or teacher thereof, as such; and that no preference shall be given to nor any discrimination made against any church, sect or creed of religion, or any form of religious faith or worship.

Section 8. Freedom of Speech—Evidence of Truth in Defamation Actions—Province of Jury

That no law shall be passed impairing the freedom of speech, no matter by what means communicated: that every person shall be free to say, write or publish, or otherwise communicate whatever he will on any subject, being responsible for all abuses of that liberty; and that in all suits and prosecutions for libel or slander the truth thereof may be given in evidence; and in suits and prosecutions for libel the jury, under the direction of the court, shall determine the law and the facts.

Section 9. Rights of Peaceable Assembly and Petition

That the people have the right peaceably to assemble for their common good, and to apply to those invested with the powers of government for redress of grievances by petition or remonstrance.

Section 10. Due Process of Law

That no person shall be deprived of life, liberty or property without due process of law.

Section 11. Imprisonment for Debt

That no person shall be imprisoned for debt, except for nonpayment of fines and penalties imposed by law.

Section 12. Habeas Corpus

That the privilege of the writ of habeas corpus shall never be suspended.

Section 13. Ex Post Facto Laws—Impairment of Contracts—Irrevocable Privileges

That no ex post facto law, nor law impairing the obligation of contracts, or retrospective in its operation, or making any irrevocable grant of special privileges or immunities, can be enacted.

Section 14. Open Courts—Certain Remedies—Justice Without Sale, Denial Or Delay

That the courts of justice shall be open to every person, and certain remedy afforded for every injury to person, property or character, and that right and justice shall be administered without sale, denial or delay.

Section 15. Unreasonable Search and Seizure Prohibited—Contents and Basis of Warrants

That the people shall be secure in their persons, papers, homes, effects, and electronic communications and data, from unreasonable searches and seizures; and no warrant to search any place, or seize any person or thing, or access electronic data or communication, shall issue without describing the place to be searched, or the person or thing to be seized, or the data or communication to be accessed, as nearly as may be; nor without probable cause, supported by written oath or affirmation.

Section 16. Grand Juries—Composition—Jurisdiction to Convene—Powers

That a grand jury shall consist of twelve citizens, any nine of whom concurring may find an indictment or a true bill: Provided, that no grand jury shall be convened except upon an order of a judge of a court having the power to try and determine felonies; but when so assembled such grand jury shall have power to investigate and return indictments for all character and grades of crime; and that the power of grand juries to inquire into the willful misconduct in office of public officers, and to find indictments in connection therewith, shall never be suspended.

Section 17. Indictments and Informations in Criminal Cases—Exceptions

That no person shall be prosecuted criminally for felony or misdemeanor otherwise than by indictment or information, which shall be concurrent remedies, but this shall not be applied to cases arising in the land or naval forces or in the militia when in actual service in time of war or public danger, nor to prevent arrests and preliminary examination in any criminal case.

Section 18(A). Rights of Accused in Criminal Prosecutions

That in criminal prosecutions the accused shall have the right to appear and defend, in person and by counsel; to demand the nature and cause of the accusation; to meet the witnesses against him face to face; to have process to compel the attendance of witnesses in his behalf; and a speedy public trial by an impartial jury of the county.

Section 18(B). Depositions in Felony Cases

Upon a hearing and finding by the circuit court in any case wherein the accused is charged with a felony, that it is necessary to take the deposition of any witness within the state, other than defendant and spouse, in order to preserve the testimony, and on condition that the court make such orders as will fully protect the rights of personal confrontation and cross-examination of the witness by defendant, the state may take the deposition of such witness and either party may use the same at the trial, as in civil cases, provided there has been substantial compliance with such orders. The reasonable personal and traveling expenses of defendant and his counsel shall be paid by the state or county as provided by law.

Section 18(C). Admissibility of Evidence

Notwithstanding the provisions of sections 17 and 18(a) of this article to the contrary, in prosecutions for crimes of a sexual nature involving a victim under eighteen years of age, relevant evidence of prior criminal acts, whether charged or uncharged, is admissible for the purpose of corroborating the victim's testimony or demonstrating the defendant's propensity to commit the crime with which he or she is presently charged. The court may exclude relevant evidence of prior criminal acts if the probative value of the evidence is substantially outweighed by the danger of unfair prejudice.

Section 19. Self-Incrimination and Double Jeopardy

That no person shall be compelled to testify against himself in a criminal cause, nor shall any person be put again in jeopardy of life or liberty for the same offense, after being once acquitted by a jury; but if the jury fail to render a verdict the court may, in its discretion, discharge the jury and commit or bail the prisoner for trial at the same or next term of court; and if judgment be arrested after a verdict of guilty on a defective indictment or information, or if judgment on a verdict of guilty be reversed for error in law, the prisoner may be tried anew on a proper indictment or information, or according to the law.

Section 20. Bail Guaranteed—Exceptions

That all persons shall be bail able by sufficient sureties, except for capital offenses, when the proof is evident or the presumption great.

Section 21. Excessive Bail and Fines—Cruel and Unusual Punishment

That excessive bail shall not be required, nor excessive fines imposed, nor cruel and unusual punishment inflicted.

Section 22(A). Right of Trial by Jury—Qualification of Jurors—Two-Thirds Verdict

That the right of trial by jury as heretofore enjoyed shall remain inviolate; provided that a jury for the trial of criminal and civil cases in courts not of record may consist of less than twelve citizens as may be prescribed by law, and a two-thirds majority of such number concurring may render a verdict in all civil cases; that in all civil cases in courts of record, three-fourths of the members of the jury concurring may render a verdict; and that in every criminal case any defendant may, with the assent of the court, waive a jury trial and submit the trial of such case to the court, whose finding shall have the force and effect of a verdict of a jury.

Section 22(B). Female Jurors—Optional Exemption

No citizen shall be disqualified from jury service because of sex, but the court shall excuse any woman who requests exemption therefrom before being sworn as a juror.

Section 23. Right to Keep and Bear Arms, Ammunition, and Certain Accessories—Exception—Rights to be Unalienable

That the right of every citizen to keep and bear arms, ammunition, and accessories typical to the normal function of such arms, in defense of his home, person, family and property, or when lawfully summoned in aid of the civil power, shall not be questioned. The rights guaranteed by this section shall be unalienable. Any restriction on these rights shall be subject to strict scrutiny and the state of Missouri shall be obligated to uphold these rights and shall under no circumstances decline to protect against their infringement. Nothing in this section shall be construed to prevent the general assembly from enacting general laws which limit the rights of convicted violent felons or those adjudicated by a court to be a danger to self or others as result of a mental disorder or mental infirmity.

Section 24. Subordination of Military to Civil Power—Quartering Soldiers

That the military shall be always in strict subordination to the civil power; that no soldier shall be quartered in any house without the consent of the owner in time of peace, nor in time of war, except as prescribed by law.

Section 25. Elections and Right of Suffrage

That all elections shall be free and open; and no power, civil or military, shall at any time interfere to prevent the free exercise of the right of suffrage.

Section 26. Compensation for Property Taken by Eminent Domain—Condemnation Juries—Payment—Railroad Property

That private property shall not be taken or damaged for public use without just compensation. Such compensation shall be ascertained by a jury or board of commissioners of not less than three freeholders, in such manner as may be provided by law; and until the same shall be paid to the owner, or into court for the owner, the property shall not be disturbed or the proprietary rights of the owner therein divested. The fee of land taken for railroad purposes without consent of the owner thereof shall remain in such owner subject to the use for which it is taken.

Section 27. Acquisition of Excess Property by Eminent Domain—Disposition Under Restrictions

That in such manner and under such limitations as may be provided by law, the state, or any county or city may acquire by eminent domain such property, or rights in property, in excess of that actually to be occupied by the public improvement or used in connection therewith, as may be reasonably necessary to effectuate the purposes intended, and may be vested with the fee simple title thereto, or the control of the use thereof, and may sell such excess property with such restrictions as shall be appropriate to preserve the improvements made.

Section 28. Limitation On Taking of Private Property for Private Use—Exceptions—Public Use A Judicial Question

That private property shall not be taken for private use with or without compensation, unless by consent of the owner, except for private ways of necessity, and except for drains and ditches across the lands of others for agricultural and sanitary purposes, in the manner prescribed by law; and that when an attempt is made to take private property for a use alleged to be public, the question whether the contemplated use be public shall be judicially determined without regard to any legislative declaration that the use is public.

Section 29.—Organized Labor and Collective Bargaining

That employees shall have the right to organize and to bargain collectively through representatives of their own choosing.

Section 30. Treason—Attainder—Corruption of Blood and Forfeitures—Estate of Suicides—Death by Casualty

That treason against the state can consist only in levying war against it, or in adhering to its enemies, giving them aid and comfort; that no person can be convicted of treason, unless on the testimony of two witnesses to the same overt act, or on his confession in open court; that no person can be attainted of treason or felony by the general assembly; that no conviction can work corruption of blood or forfeiture of estate; that the estates of such persons as may destroy their own lives shall descend or vest as in cases of natural death; and when any person shall be killed by casualty, there shall be no forfeiture by reason thereof.

Section 31. Fines Or Imprisonments Fixed by Administrative Agencies

That no law shall delegate to any commission, bureau, board or other administrative agency authority to make any rule fixing a fine or imprisonment as punishment for its violation.

Section 32. Crime Victims Rights

1. Crime victims, as defined by law, shall have the following rights, as defined by law:

(1) The right to be present at all criminal justice proceedings at which the defendant has such right, including juvenile proceedings where the offense would have been a felony if committed by an adult;

(2) Upon request of the victim, the right to be informed of and heard at guilty pleas, bail hearings, sentencings, probation revocation hearings, and parole hearings, unless in the determination of the court the interests of justice require otherwise;

(3) The right to be informed of trials and preliminary hearings;

(4) The right to restitution, which shall be enforceable in the same manner as any other civil cause of action, or as otherwise provided by law;

(5) The right to the speedy disposition and appellate review of their cases, provided that nothing in this subdivision shall prevent the defendant from having sufficient time to prepare his defense;

(6) The right to reasonable protection from the defendant or any person acting on behalf of the defendant;

(7) The right to information concerning the escape of an accused from custody or confinement, the defendant's release and scheduling of the defendant's release from incarceration; and

(8) The right to information about how the criminal justice system works, the rights and the availability of services, and upon request of the victim the right to information about the crime.

2. Notwithstanding section 20 of article I of this Constitution, upon a showing that the defendant poses a danger to a crime victim, the community, or any other person, the court may deny bail or may impose special conditions which the defendant and surety must guarantee.

3. Nothing in this section shall be construed as creating a cause of action for money damages against the state, a county, a municipality, or any of the agencies, instrumentalities, or employees provided that the General Assembly may, by statutory enactment, reverse, modify, or supersede any judicial decision or rule arising from any cause of action brought pursuant to this section.

4. Nothing in this section shall be construed to authorize a court to set aside or to void a finding of guilt, or an acceptance of a plea of guilty in any criminal case.

5. The general assembly shall have power to enforce this section by appropriate legislation.

Section 33. Marriage, Validity and Recognition

That to be valid and recognized in this state, a marriage shall exist only between a man and a woman.

Section 34. English to be the Official Language in This State

That English shall be the language of all official proceedings in this state. Official proceedings shall be limited to any meeting of a public governmental body at which any public business is discussed, decided, or public policy formulated, whether such meeting is conducted in person or by means of communication equipment, including, but not limited to, conference call, video conference, Internet chat, or Internet message board. The term "official proceeding" shall not include an informal gathering of members of a public governmental body for ministerial or social purposes, but the term shall include a public vote of all or a majority of the members of a public governmental body, by electronic communication or any other means, conducted in lieu of holding an official proceeding with the members of the public governmental body gathered at one location in order to conduct public business.

Section 35. Right to Farm

That agriculture which provides food, energy, health benefits, and security is the foundation and stabilizing force of Missouri's economy. to protect this vital sector of Missouri's economy, the right of farmers and ranchers to engage in farming and ranching practices shall be forever guaranteed in this state, subject to duly authorized powers, if any, conferred by article VI of the Constitution of Missouri.

ARTICLE II: THE DISTRIBUTION OF POWERS

Section 1. Three Departments of Government—Separation of Powers

The powers of government shall be divided into three distinct departments—the legislative, executive and judicial—each of which shall be confided to a separate magistracy, and no person, or collection of persons, charged with the exercise of powers properly belonging to one of those departments, shall exercise any power properly belonging to either of the others, except in the instances in this constitution expressly directed or permitted.

ARTICLE III: LEGISLATIVE DEPARTMENT

Section 1. Legislative Power—General Assembly

The legislative power shall be vested in a senate and house of representatives to be styled "The General Assembly of the State of Missouri."

Section 2. Election of Representatives—Apportionment Commission, Appointment, Duties, Compensation

The house of representatives shall consist of one hundred sixty-three members elected at each general election and apportioned in the following manner: Within sixty days after the population of this state is reported to the President for each decennial census of the United States and, in the event that a reapportionment has been invalidated by a court of competent jurisdiction, within sixty days after notification by the gov ernor that such a ruling has been made, the congressional district committee of each of the two parties casting the highest vote for governor at the last preceding election shall meet and the members of the committee shall nominate, by a majority vote of the members of the committee present, provided that a majority of the elected members is present, two members of their party, residents in that district, as nominees for reapportionment commissioners. Neither party shall select more than one nominee from any one state legislative district. The congressional committees shall each submit to the governor their list of elected nominees. Within thirty days the governor shall appoint a commission consisting of one name from each list to reapportion the state into one hundred and sixty-three representative districts and to establish the numbers and boundaries of said districts. If any of the congressional committees fails to submit a list within such time the governor shall appoint a member of his own choice from that district and from the political party of the committee failing to make the appointment. Members of the commission shall be disqualified from holding office as members of the general assembly for four years following the date of the filing by the commission of its final statement of apportionment. for the purposes of this article, the term congressional district committee or congressional district refers to the congressional district committee or the congressional district from which a congressman was last elected, or, in the event members of congress from this state have been elected at large, the term congressional district committee refers to those persons who last served as the congressional district committee for those districts from which congressmen were last elected, and the term congressional district refers to those districts from which congressmen were last elected. Any action pursuant to this section by the congressional district committee shall take place only at duly called meetings, shall be recorded in their official minutes and only members present in person shall be permitted to vote. The commissioners so selected shall on the fifteenth day, excluding Sun days and holidays, after all members have been selected, meet in the capitol building and proceed to organize by electing from their number a chairman, vice chairman and secretary and shall adopt an agenda establishing at least three hearing dates on which hearings open to the public shall be held. A copy of the agenda shall be filed with the clerk of the house of representatives within twenty-four hours after its adoption. Executive meetings may be scheduled and held as often as the commission deems advisable. The commission shall reapportion the representatives by dividing the population of the state by the number one hundred sixty-three and shall establish each district so that the population of that district shall, as nearly as possible, equal that figure. Each district shall be composed of contiguous territory as compact as may be. Not later than five months after the appointment of the commission, the com mission shall file with the secretary of state a tentative plan of apportionment and map of the proposed districts and during the ensuing fifteen days shall hold such public hearings as may be necessary to hear objections or testimony of interested persons. Not later than six months after the appointment of the commission, the commission shall file with the secretary of state a final statement of the numbers and the boundaries of the districts together with a map of the districts, and no statement shall be valid unless approved by at least seven-tenths of the members. After the statement is filed members of the house of representatives shall be elected according to such districts until a reapportionment is made as herein provided, except that if the statement is not filed within six months of the time fixed for the appointment of the commission, it shall stand discharged and the house of representatives shall be apportioned by a commission of six members appointed from among the judges of the appellate courts of the state of Missouri by the state supreme court, a majority of whom shall sign and file its apportionment plan and map with the secretary of state within ninety days of the date of the discharge of the apportionment commission. Thereafter members of the house of representatives shall be elected according to such districts until a reapportionment is made as herein provided. Each member of the commission shall receive as compensation fifteen dollars a day for each day the commission is in session but not more than one thousand dollars, and, in addition, shall be reimbursed for his actual and necessary expenses incurred while serving as a member of the commission. No reapportionment shall be subject to the referendum.

Section 3. Repealed

Section 4. Qualifications of Representatives

Each representative shall be twenty-four years of age, and next before the day of his election shall have been a qualified voter for two years and a resident of the county or district which he is chosen to represent for one year, if such county or district shall have been so long established, and if not, then of the county or district from which the same shall have been taken.

Section 5. Senators—Number—Senatorial Districts

The Senate shall consist of thirty-four members elected by the qualified voters of the respective districts for four years. for the election of senators, the state shall be divided into convenient districts of contiguous territory, as compact and nearly equal in population as may be.

Section 6. Qualifications of Senators

Each senator shall be thirty years of age, and next before the day of his election shall have been a qualified voter of the state for three years and a resident of the district which he is chosen to represent for one year, if such district shall have been so long established, and if not, then of the district or districts from which the same shall have been taken.

Section 7. Senatorial Apportionment Commission—Number, Appointment, Duties, Compensation

Within sixty days after the population of this state is reported to the President for each decennial census of the United States, and within sixty days after notification by the governor that a reapportionment has been invalidated by a court of competent jurisdiction, the state committee of each of the two political parties casting the highest vote for governor at the last preceding election shall, at a committee meeting duly called, select by a vote of the individual committee members, and thereafter submit to the governor a list of ten persons, and within thirty days thereafter the governor shall appoint a commission of ten members, five from each list, to reapportion the thirty-four senatorial districts and to establish the numbers and boundaries of said districts. If either of the party committees fails to submit a list within such time the governor shall appoint five members of his own choice from the party of the committee so failing to act. Members of the commission shall be disqualified from holding office as members of the general assembly for four years following the date of the filing by the commission of its final statement of apportionment.

The commissioners so selected shall on the fifteenth day, excluding Sundays and holidays, after all members have been selected, meet in the capitol building and proceed to organize by electing from their number a chairman, vice chairman and secretary and shall adopt an agenda establishing at least three hearing dates on which hearings open to the public shall be held. A copy of the agenda shall be filed with the secretary of the senate within twenty-four hours after its adoption. Executive meetings may be scheduled and held as often as the commission deems advisable. The commission shall reapportion the senatorial districts by dividing the population of the state by the number thirty-four and shall establish each district so that the population of that district shall, as nearly as possible, equal that figure; no county lines shall be crossed except when necessary to add sufficient population to a multi-district county or city to complete only one district which lies partly within such multi-district county or city so as to be as nearly equal as practicable in population. Any county with a population in excess of the quotient obtained by dividing the population of the state by the number thirty-four is hereby declared to be a multi-district county. Not later than five months after the appointment of the commission, the commission shall file with the secretary of state a tentative plan of apportionment and map of the proposed districts and during the ensuing fifteen days shall hold such public hearings as may be necessary to hear objections or testimony of interested persons. Not later than six months after the appointment of the commission, the commission shall file with the secretary of state a final statement of the numbers and the boundaries of the districts together with a map of the districts, and no statement shall be valid unless approved by at least seven members. After the statement is filed senators shall be elected according to such districts until a reapportionment is made as herein provided, except that if the statement is not filed within six months of the time fixed for the appointment of the commission, it shall stand discharged and the senate shall be apportioned by a commission of six members appointed from among the judges of the appellate courts of the state of Missouri by the state supreme court, a majority of whom shall sign and file its apportionment plan and map with the secretary of state within ninety days of the date of the discharge of the apportionment commission. Thereafter senators shall be elected according to such districts until a reapportionment is made as herein provided. Each member of the commission shall receive as compensation fifteen dollars a day for each day the commission is in session, but not more than one thousand dollars, and, in addition, shall be reimbursed for his actual and necessary expenses incurred while serving as a member of the commission. No reapportionment shall be subject to the referendum.

Section 8. Term Limitations for Members of General Assembly

No one shall be elected to serve more than eight years total in any one house of the General Assembly nor more than sixteen years total in both houses of the General Assembly. in applying this section, service in the General Assembly resulting from an election prior to December 3, 1992, or service of less than one year, in the case of a member of the house of representatives, or two years, in the case of a member of the senate, by a person elected after the effective date of this section to complete the term of another person, shall not be counted.

Section 9. Apportionment of Representatives

Until the convening of the Seventy-fourth General Assembly the House of Representatives shall consist of one hundred sixty-three members elected from the one hundred sixty-three representative districts, as they existed January 1, 1965.

Section 10. Basis of Apportionment—Alteration of Districts

The last decennial census of the United States shall be used in apportioning representatives and determining the population of senatorial and representative districts. Such districts may be altered from time to time as public convenience may require.

Section 11. Time of Election of Senators and Representatives

The first election of senators and representatives under this constitution, shall be held at the general election in the year one thousand nine hundred and forty-six when the whole number of representatives and the senators from the districts having even numbers, who shall compose the first class, shall be elected, and two years thereafter the whole number of representatives and the senators from districts having odd numbers, who shall compose the second class, shall be elected, and so on at each succeeding general election.

Section 12. Members of General Assembly Disqualified From Holding Other Offices

No person holding any lucrative office or employment under the United States, this state or any municipality thereof shall hold the office of senator or representative. When any senator or representative accepts any office or employment under the United States, this state or any municipality thereof, his office shall thereby be vacated and he shall thereafter perform no duty and receive no salary as senator or representative. During the term for which he was elected no senator or representative shall accept any appointive office or employment under this state which is created or the emoluments of which are increased during such term. This section shall not apply to members of the organized militia, of the reserve corps and of school boards, and notaries public.

Section 13. Vacation of Office by Removal of Residence

If any senator or representative remove his residence from the district or county for which he was elected, his office shall thereby be vacated.

Section 14. Writs of Election to Fill Vacancies

Writs of election to fill vacancies in either house of the general assembly shall be issued by the governor.

Section 15. Oath of Office of Members of Assembly—Administration—Effect of Refusal to Take Oath and Conviction of Violation

Every senator or representative elect, before entering upon the duties of his office, shall take and subscribe the following oath or affirmation: "I do solemnly swear, or affirm, that I will support the Constitution of the United States and of the state of Missouri, and faithfully perform the duties of my office, and that I will not knowingly receive, directly or indirectly, any money or other valuable thing for the performance or nonperformance of any act or duty pertaining to my office, other than the compensation allowed by law." The oath shall be administered in the halls of the respective houses to the members thereof, by a judge of the supreme court or a circuit court, or after the organization by the presiding officer of either house, and shall be filed in the office of the secretary of state. Any senator or representative refusing to take said oath or affirmation shall be deemed to have vacated his office, and any member convicted of having violated his oath or affirmation shall be deemed guilty of perjury, and be forever disqualified from holding any office of trust or profit in this state.

Section 16. Compensation, Mileage Allowance and Expenses of General Assembly Members

Senators and representatives shall receive from the state treasury as salary such sums as are provided by law. No law fixing the compensation of members of the general assembly shall become effective un til the first day of the regular session of the general assembly next following the session at which the law was enacted. Upon certification by the president and secretary of the senate and by the speaker and chief clerk of the house of representatives as to the respective members thereof, the state comptroller shall audit and the state treasurer shall pay such compensation without legislative enactment. Until otherwise provided by law senators and representatives shall receive one dollar for every ten miles traveled in going to and re turning from their place of meeting while the legislature is in session, on the most usual route. Until otherwise provided by law, each senator or representative shall be reimbursed from the state treasury for the actual and necessary expenses incurred by him in attending sessions of the general assembly in the sum of ten dollars ($10.00) per day for each day on which the journal of the senate or house respectively shows the presence of such senator or representative. Upon certification by the president and secretary of the senate and by the speaker and chief clerk of the house of representatives as to the respective members thereof, the state comptroller shall approve and the state treasurer shall pay monthly such expense allowance without legislative enactment.

Section 17. Limitation On Number of Legislative Employees

Until otherwise provided by law, the house of representatives shall not employ more than one hundred twenty-five and the senate shall not employ more than seventy-five employees elective, appointive or any other at any time during any session.

Section 18. Appointment of Officers of Houses—Jurisdiction to Determine Membership—Power to Make Rules, Punish for Contempt and Disorderly Conduct and Expel Members

Each house shall appoint its own officers; shall be sole judge of the qualifications, election and returns of its own members; may determine the rules of its own proceedings, except as herein provided; may arrest and punish by fine not exceeding three hundred dollars, or imprisonment in a county jail not exceeding ten days, or both, any person not a member, who shall be guilty of disrespect to the house by any disorderly or contemptuous behavior in its presence during its sessions; may punish its members for disorderly conduct; and, with the concurrence of two-thirds of all members elect, may expel a member; but no member shall be expelled a second time for the same cause.

Section 19. Legislative Privileges

Senators and representatives shall, in all cases except treason, felony, or breach of the peace, be privileged from arrest during the session of the general assembly, and for the fifteen days next be fore the commencement and after the termination of each session; and they shall not be questioned for any speech or debate in either house in any other place.

Section 20. Regular Sessions of Assembly—Quorum— Compulsory At Ten Dance— Public Sessions—Limitation On Power to Adjourn

The general assembly shall meet on the first Wednesday after the first Monday in January following each general election. The general assembly may provide by law for the introduction of bills during the period between the first day of December and the first Wednesday after the first Monday of January. The general assembly shall reconvene on the first Wednesday after the first Monday of January after adjournment at midnight on May thirtieth of the preceding year. A majority of the elected members of each house shall constitute a quorum to do business, but a smaller number may adjourn from day to day, and may compel the attendance of absent members in such manner and under such penalties as each house may provide. The sessions of each house shall be held with open doors, except in cases which may require secrecy but not including the final vote on bills, resolutions and confirmations. Neither house shall, without the consent of the other, adjourn for more than ten days at any one time, nor to any other place than that in which the two houses may be sitting.

Section 20(A). Automatic Adjournment—Tabling of Bills, When

The general assembly shall adjourn at midnight on May thirtieth until the first Wednesday after the first Monday of January of the following year, unless it has adjourned prior thereto. All bills in either house remaining on the calendar after 6:00 pm. on the first Friday following the second Monday in May are tabled. The period between the first Friday following the second Monday in May and May thirtieth shall be devoted to the enrolling, engrossing, and the signing in open session by officers of the respective houses of bills passed prior to 6:00 pm. on the first Friday following the second Monday in May. The general assembly shall automatically stand adjourned sine die at 6:00 pm. on the sixtieth calendar day after the date of its convening in special session unless it has adjourned sine die prior thereto.

Section 20(B). Special Session, Procedure to Convene—Limitations—Automatic Adjournment

Upon the filing with the secretary of state of a petition stating the purpose for which the session is to be called and signed by three-fourths of the members of the senate and three-fourths of the members of the house of representatives, the president pro tem of the senate and the speaker of the house shall by joint proclamation convene the general assembly in special session. The proclamation shall state specifically each matter contained in the petition on which action is deemed necessary. No appropriation bill shall be considered in a special session convened pursuant to this section if in that year the general assembly has not passed the operating budget in compliance with Section 25 of this article. The general assembly shall automatically stand adjourned sine die at 6:00 pm. on the thirtieth calendar day after the date of its convening in special session under this section unless it has adjourned sine die prior thereto.

LEGISLATIVE PROCEEDINGS:

Section 21. Style of Laws—Bills—Limitation On Amendments—Power of Each House to Originate and Amend Bills—Reading of Bills

The style of the laws of this state shall be: "be it enacted by the General Assembly of the State of Missouri, as follows." No law shall be passed except by bill, and no bill shall be so amended in its passage through either house as to change its original purpose. Bills may originate in either house and may be amended or rejected by the other. Every bill shall be read by title on three different days in each house.

Section 22. Referral of Bills to Committees—Recall of Referred Bills—Records of Committees—Provision for Interim Meetings

Every bill shall be referred to a committee of the house in which it is pending. After it has been referred to a committee, one-third of the elected members of the respective houses shall have power to relieve a committee of further consideration of a bill and place it on the calendar for consideration. Each committee shall keep such record of its proceedings as is required by rule of the respective houses and this record and the recorded vote of the members of the committee shall be filed with all reports on bills. Each house of the general assembly may provide by rule for such committees of that house as it deems necessary to meet to consider bills or to perform any other necessary legislative function during the interim between the session ending on the thirtieth day of May and the session commencing on the first Wednesday after the first Monday of January.

Section 23. Limitation of Scope of Bills—Contents of Titles—Exceptions

No bill shall contain more than one subject which shall be clearly expressed in its title, except bills enacted under the third exception in section 37 of this article and general appropriation bills, which may embrace the various subjects and accounts for which moneys are appropriated.

Section 24. Printing of Bills and Amendments

No bill shall be considered for final passage in either house until it, with all amendments thereto, has been printed and copies distributed among the members. If a bill passed by either house be returned thereto, amended by the other, the house to which the same is returned shall cause the amendment or amendments so received to be printed and copies distributed among the members before final action on such amendments.

Section 25. Limitation On Introduction of Bills

No bill other than an appropriation bill shall be introduced in either house after the sixtieth legislative day unless consented to by a majority of the elected members of each house or the governor shall request a consideration of the proposed legislation by a special message. No appropriation bill shall be taken up for consideration after 6:00 pm. on the first Friday following the first Monday in May of each year.

Section 26. Legislative Journals—Demand for Yeas and Nays—Manner and Record of Vote

Each house shall publish a journal of its proceedings. The yeas and nays on any question shall be taken and entered on the journal on the motion of any five members. Whenever the yeas and nays are demanded, or required by this constitution, the whole list of members shall be called and the names of the members voting yea and nay and the absentees shall be entered in the journal.

Section 27. Concurrence in Amendments—Adoption of Conference Committee Reports—Final Passage of Bills

No amendments to bills by one house shall be concurred in by the other, nor shall reports of committees of conference be adopted in either house, nor shall a bill be finally passed, unless a vote by yeas and nays be taken and a majority of the members elected to each house be recorded as voting favorably.

Section 28. Form of Reviving, Reenacting and Amending Bills

No act shall be revived or reenacted unless it shall be set forth at length as if it were an original act. No act shall be amended by providing that words be stricken out or inserted, but the words to be stricken out, or the words to be inserted, or the words to be stricken out and those inserted in lieu thereof, together with the act or section amended, shall be set forth in full as amended.

Section 29. Effective Date of Laws—Exceptions—Procedure in Emergencies and Upon Recess

No law passed by the general assembly, except an appropriation act, shall take effect until ninety days after the adjournment of the session in either odd-numbered or even-numbered years at which it was enacted. However, in case of an emergency which must be expressed in the preamble or in the body of the act, the general assembly by a two-thirds vote of the members elected to each house, taken by yeas and nays may otherwise direct; and further except that, if the general assembly recess es for thirty days or more it may prescribe by joint resolution that laws previously passed and not effective shall take effect ninety days from the beginning of the recess.

Section 30. Signing of Bills by Presiding Officers— Procedure On Objections— Presentation of Bills to Governor

No bill shall become a law until it is signed by the presiding officer of each house in open session, who first shall suspend all other business, declare that the bill shall now be read and that if no objection be made he will sign the same. If in either house any member shall object in writing to the signing of a bill, the objection shall be noted in the journal and annexed to the bill to be considered by the governor in connection therewith. When a bill has been signed, the secretary, or the chief clerk, of the house in which the bill originated shall present the bill in person to the governor on the same day on which it was signed and enter the fact upon the journal.

Section 31. Governor's Duty As to Bills and Joint Resolutions—Time Limitations—Failure to Return, Bill Becomes Law

Every bill which shall have passed the house of representatives and the senate shall be presented to and considered by the governor, and, within fifteen days after presentment, he shall return such bill to the house in which it originated endorsed with his approval or accompanied by his objections. If the bill be approved by the governor it shall become a law. When the general assembly adjourns, or recesses for a period of thirty days or more, the governor shall return within forty-five days any bill to the office of the secretary of state with his approval or reasons for disapproval. If any bill shall not be returned by the governor within the time limits prescribed by this section it shall become law in like manner as if the governor had signed it.

Section 32. Vetoed Bills Reconsidered, When

Every bill presented to the governor and returned with his objections shall stand as reconsidered in the house to which it is returned. If the governor returns any bill with his objections on or after the fifth day before the last day upon which a session of the general assembly may consider bills, the general assembly shall automatically reconvene on the first Wednesday following the second Monday in September for a period not to exceed ten calendar days for the sole purpose of considering bills returned by the governor. The objections of the governor shall be entered upon the journal and the house shall proceed to consider the question pending, which shall be in this form: "Shall the bill pass, the objections of the governor thereto notwithstanding?" The vote upon this question shall be taken by yeas and nays and if two-thirds of the elected members of the house vote in the affirmative the presiding officer of that house shall certify that fact on the roll, attesting the same by his signature, and send the bill with the objections of the governor to the other house, in which like proceedings shall be had in relation thereto. The bill thus certified shall be deposited in the office of the secretary of state as an authentic act and shall become a law.

Section 33. Repealed

Section 34. Revision of General Statutes—Limitation On Compensation

in the year 1949 and at least every ten years thereafter all general statute laws shall be revised, digested and promulgated as provided by law. No senator or representative shall receive any compensation in addition to his salary as a member of the general assembly for any services rendered in connection with said revision.

Section 35. Committee On Legislative Research

There shall be a permanent joint committee on legislative research, selected by and from the members of each house as provided by law. The general assembly, by a majority vote of the elected members, may discharge any or all of the members of the committee at any time and select their successors. The committee may employ a staff as provided by law. The committee shall meet when necessary to perform the duties, advisory to the general assembly, assigned to it by law. The members of the committee shall receive no compensation in addition to their salary as members of the general assembly, but may receive their necessary expenses while attending the meetings of the committee.

LIMITATION OF LEGISLATIVE POWER

Section 36. Payment of State Revenues and Receipts to Treasury—Limitation of Withdrawals to Appropriations—Order of Appropriations

All revenue collected and money received by the state shall go into the treasury and the general assembly shall have no power to divert the same or to permit the withdrawal of money from the treasury, except in pursuance of appropriations made by law. All appropriations of money by successive general assemblies shall be made in the following order:

First: for payment of sinking fund and interest on outstanding obligations of the state.

Second: for the purpose of public education.

Third: for the payment of the cost of assessing and collecting the revenue.

Fourth: for the payment of the civil lists.

Fifth: for the support of eleemosynary and other state institutions.

Sixth: for public health and public welfare.

Seventh: for all other state purposes. Eighth: for the expense of the general assembly.

Section 37. Limitation On State Debts and Bond Issues

The general assembly shall have no power to contract or authorize the contracting of any liability of the state, or to issue bonds therefor, except

(1) to refund outstanding bonds, the refunding bonds to mature not more than twenty-five years from date,

(2) on the recommendation of the governor, for a temporary liability to be incurred by reason of unforeseen emergency or casual deficiency in revenue, in a sum not to exceed one million dollars for any one year and to be paid in not more than five years from its creation, and

(3) when the liability exceeds one million dollars, the general assembly as on constitutional amendments, or the people by the initiative, may also submit a measure containing the amount, purpose and terms of the liability, and if the measure is approved by a majority of the qualified electors of the state voting thereon at the election, the liability may be incurred, and the bonds issued therefor must be re tired serially and by installments within a period not exceeding twenty-five years from their date. Before any bonds are issued under this section the general assembly shall make adequate provision for the payment of the principal and interest, and may provide an annual tax on all taxable property in an amount sufficient for the purpose.

Section 37(A). State Building Bond Issue Authorized—Interest Rate—Pay Ment From Income Tax and Other Funds

in addition to the exceptions made in Section 37, the General Assembly shall have power to contract, or to authorize the contracting of, a debt or liability on behalf of the state, and to is sue bonds or other evidence of indebtedness therefor, not exceeding in the aggregate Seventy-five Million Dollars ($75,000,000), for the purpose of re pair ing, remodeling or rebuilding, or of repairing, remodeling and rebuilding state buildings and properties at all or any of the penal, correctional and reformatory institutions of this state, the state training schools, state hospitals and state schools and other eleemosynary institutions of this state, and institutions of higher education of this state, and for building additions thereto and additional buildings where necessary, and for furnishing and equipping any such improvements.

Such bonds shall bear interest at a rate not exceeding three percentum (3%) per annum, payable semiannually, except that the first interest payable thereon may be paid not later than one year from the date of issuance, and maturing not later than twenty-five years from their date. Such bonds shall be issued by the State Board of Fund Commissioners in such amount, from time to time, as may be necessary to carry on the building program as determined by the General Assembly. The proceeds of the sale or sales of any bonds issued hereunder shall be paid into the state treasury and be credited to a fund to be designated the "Second State Building Fund."

The proceeds of the sale of the bonds herein authorized shall be expended for the purposes for which the bonds are hereinabove authorized to be issued.

The bonds and the interest thereon shall be paid out of the Second State Building Bond Interest and Sinking Fund, which is hereby created. Upon the issuance of such bonds, or any portion thereof, the State Board of Fund Com missioners shall notify the State Comptroller of the amount of money required, in the remaining portion of the fiscal year during which said bonds shall have been issued, for the payment of interest on the said bonds, and of the amount of money required for the payment of interest on the said bonds in the next succeeding fiscal year, and for the establishment and maintenance of a sinking fund to pay said bonds as they mature. Thereafter, within thirty days after the beginning of each fiscal year, the State Board of Fund Commissioners shall notify the State Comptroller of the amount of money required for the payment of interest on the said bonds in the next succeeding fiscal year and for the maintenance of the sinking fund to pay said bonds maturing in such next succeeding fiscal year.

It shall be the duty of the State Comptroller to transfer, at least monthly, the proceeds of the state income tax, after deducting therefrom the proportionate part thereof appropriated for the support of the free public schools, to the credit of the Second State Building Bond Interest and Sinking Fund until there shall have been transferred to said fund the amount so certified to him by the State Board of Fund Commissioners, as hereinabove provided.

If at any time after the issuance of any of the said bonds, it shall become apparent to the State Comptroller that the proceeds of the state income tax, as aforesaid, will not be sufficient for the payment of the principal and interest maturing and accruing on said bonds during the next succeeding fiscal year, a direct tax shall be levied upon all taxable tangible property in the state for the payment of said bonds and the interest that will accrue thereon. in such event, it shall be the duty of the State Comptroller annually, on or before the first day of July, to determine the rate of taxation necessary to be levied upon all taxable tangible property within the state to raise the amount of money needed to pay the principal of and interest on such bonds maturing and accruing in the next succeeding fiscal year, taking into consideration available funds, delinquencies and costs of collection. The State Comptroller shall annually certify the rate of taxation so determined to the county clerk of each county and to the comptroller or other officer in the city of St. Louis whose duty it shall be to make up and certify the tax books wherein are extended the ad valorem state taxes. It shall be the duty of said clerks and the said comptroller or other proper officer in the city of St. Louis to extend upon the tax books the taxes to be collected and to certify the same to the collectors of the revenue of their respective counties and of the city of St. Louis, who shall collect such taxes at the same time and in the same manner and by the same means as are now or may hereafter be provided by law for the collection of state and county taxes, and to pay the same into the state treasury for the credit of the Second State Building Bond Interest and Sinking Fund.

If at any time the balance in said Second State Building Bond Interest and Sinking Fund should be insufficient to pay accruing interest or maturing principal of said bonds, the Board of Fund Commissioners shall direct the State Comptroller to transfer from the State Revenue Fund to said Second State Building Bond Interest and Sinking Fund the sum required for said purposes, or either of them, and said sum so transferred shall be reimbursed to the State Revenue Fund whenever there may be a balance in the Second State Building Bond Interest and Sinking Fund in excess of the amount which may then be needed to meet the accruing interest and maturing principal of the said bonds during one fiscal year next succeeding.

All funds paid into the Second State Building Bond Interest and Sinking Fund shall be and stand appropriated without legislative action to the payment of principal and interest of the said bonds, there to remain until paid out in discharge of the principal of said bonds and the interest accruing thereon, and no part of such fund shall be used for any other purpose so long as any of the principal of said bonds and the interest thereon shall be unpaid, provided, however, that nothing herein contained shall prevent the reimbursement from the said Second State Building Bond Interest and Sinking Fund of the State Revenue Fund, as hereinabove provided.

The General Assembly shall enact such laws as may be necessary to carry this amendment into effect.

Section 37(B). Water Pollution Control Fund Established —Bonds Authorized— Funds to Stand Appropriated

The general assembly may authorize the contracting of an indebtedness on behalf of the state of Missouri and the issuance of bonds or other evidences of indebtedness not exceeding in the aggregate the sum of one hundred fifty million dollars for the purpose of providing funds for use in this state for the protection of the environment through the control of water pollution. The bonds shall be issued by the state board of fund commissioners from time to time and in such amounts as may be necessary to carry on a program by the water pollution board of the state as determined by the general assembly for the planning, financing and constructing sewage treatment facilities by any county, municipality, sewer district, or any combination of the same and the board of fund commissioners shall offer such bonds at public sale, and shall provide such method as it may deem necessary for the advertisement of the sale of each issue of said bonds before the same are sold.

The proceeds of the sale or sales of any bonds issued hereunder shall be paid into the state treasury and be credited to a fund to be designated the "Water Pollution Control Fund".

The bonds shall be retired serially and by installments within a period not to exceed twenty-five years from their date of issue and shall bear interest at a rate or rates not exceeding the rate permitted by law.

The proceeds of the sale of the bonds herein authorized shall be expended for the purposes for which the bonds are hereinabove authorized to be issued.

The bonds and the interest thereon shall be paid out of the "Water Pollution Control Bond and Interest Fund", which is hereby created, and the payment of said bonds and the interest thereon shall be secured by a pledge of the full faith, credit and resources of the state of Missouri. Upon the issuance of such bonds, or any portion thereof, the state board of fund commissioners shall notify the state comptroller of the amount of money required, in the remaining portion of the fiscal year during which said bonds shall have been issued, for the payment of interest on the said bonds, and of the amount of money required for the payment of interest on the said bonds in the next succeeding fiscal year, and to pay said bonds as they mature. Thereafter, within thirty days after the beginning of each fiscal year, the state board of fund commissioners shall notify the state comptroller of the amount of money required for the payment of interest on the said bonds in the next succeeding fiscal year and to pay said bonds maturing in such next succeeding fiscal year.

It shall be the duty of the state comptroller to transfer, at least monthly, from the state revenue fund, after deducting therefrom the proportionate part thereof appropriated for the support of the free public schools, and to credit to the water pollution control bond and interest fund such sum as may be necessary from time to time until there shall have been transferred to said fund the amount so certified to him by the state board of fund commissioners, as hereinabove provided.

If at any time after the issuance of any of the said bonds, it shall become apparent to the state comptroller that the funds available in the state revenue fund, as aforesaid, will not be sufficient for the payment of the sinking fund and interest on outstanding obligations of the state and for the purpose of public education and the principal and interest maturing and accruing on said bonds during the next succeeding fiscal year, a direct tax shall be levied upon all taxable tangible property in the state for the payment of said bonds and the interest that will accrue thereon. in such event, it shall be the duty of the state comptroller annually, on or before the first day of July, to determine the rate of taxation necessary to be levied upon all taxable tangible property within the state to raise the amount of money needed to pay the principal of and interest on such bonds maturing and accruing in the next succeeding fiscal year, taking into consideration available funds, delinquencies and costs of collection. The state comptroller shall annually certify the rate of taxation so determined to the county clerk of each county and to the comptroller or other officer in the city of St. Louis whose duty it shall be to make up and certify the tax books wherein are extended the ad valorem state taxes. It shall be the duty of said clerks and the said comptroller or other proper officer in the city of St. Louis to extend upon the tax books the taxes to be collected and to certify the same to the collectors of the revenue of their respective counties and of the city of St. Louis, who shall collect such taxes at the same time and in the same manner and by the same means as are now or may hereafter be provided by law for the collection of state and county taxes, and to pay the same into the state treasury for the credit of the water pollution control bond and interest fund. All funds paid into the water pollution control bond and interest fund shall be and stand appropriated without legislative action to the payment of principal and interest of the said bonds, there to remain until paid out in discharge of the principal of said bonds and the interest accruing thereon, and no part of such fund shall be used for any other purpose so long as any of the principal of said bonds and the interest thereon shall be unpaid.

The general assembly may enact such laws as may be necessary to carry this amendment into effect.

Section 37(C). Additional Water Pollution Control Bonds Authorized—Procedure

The general assembly may authorize the contracting of an indebtedness on behalf of the state of Missouri and the issuance of bonds or other evidences of indebtedness not exceeding in the aggregate the sum of two hundred million dollars for the purpose of providing funds for use in this state for the protection of the environment through the control of water pollution. The bonds shall be issued by the State Board of Fund Commissioners from time to time and in such amounts as may be necessary to carry on a program by the Clean Water Commission of the state as determined by the General Assembly for the planning, financing and constructing sewage treatment facilities by any county, municipality, sewer district, or any combination of the same and the Board of Fund Commissioners shall offer such bonds at public sale, and shall provide such method as it may deem necessary for the advertisement of the sale of each issue of said bonds before the same are sold.

The proceeds of the sale or sales of any bonds issued hereunder shall be paid into the state treasury and be credited to a fund to be designated the "Water Pollution Control Fund." The bonds shall be retired serially and by installments within a period not to exceed twenty-five years from their date of issue and shall bear interest at a rate or rates not exceeding the rate permitted by law. The proceeds of the sale of the bonds herein authorized shall be expended for the purposes for which the bonds are hereinabove authorized to be issued.

The bonds and the interest thereon shall be paid out of the Water Pollution Control Bond and Interest Fund, which is hereby created, and the payment of said bonds and the interest thereon shall be secured by a pledge of the full faith, credit and resources of the State of Missouri.
Upon the issuance of such bonds, or any portion thereof, the State Board of Fund Commissioners shall notify the Commissioner of Administration of the amount of money required, in the remaining portion of the fiscal year during which said bonds shall have been issued, for the payment of interest on the said bonds, and of the amount of money required for the payment of interest on the said bonds in the next succeeding fiscal year, and to pay said bonds as they mature. Thereafter, within thirty days after the beginning of each fiscal year, the State Board of Fund Commissioners shall notify the Commissioner of Administration of the amount of money required for the payment of interest on the said bonds in the next succeeding fiscal year and to pay said bonds maturing in such next succeeding fiscal year.

It shall be the duty of the Commissioner of Administration to transfer at least monthly, from the State Revenue Fund, after deducting therefrom the proportionate part thereof appropriated for the support of the free public schools, and to credit to the Water Pollution Control Bond and Interest Fund such sum as may be necessary from time to time until there shall have been transferred to said fund the amount so certified to him by the State Board of Fund Commissioners, as hereinabove provided.

If at any time after the issuance of any of the said bonds, it shall become apparent to the Commissioner of Administration that the funds available in the State Revenue Fund, as aforesaid, will not be sufficient for the payment of the sinking fund and interest on outstanding obligations of the state and for the purpose of public education and the principal and interest maturing and accruing on said bonds during the next succeeding fiscal year, a direct tax shall be levied upon all taxable tangible property in the state for the payment of said bonds and the interest that will accrue thereon. in such event, it shall be the duty of the Commissioner of Administration annually, on or before the first day of July, to determine the rate of taxation necessary to be levied upon all taxable tangible property within the state to raise the amount of money needed to pay the principal of and interest on such bonds maturing and accruing in the next succeeding fiscal year, taking into consideration available funds, delinquencies and costs of collection. The Commissioner of Administration shall annually certify the rate of taxation so determined to the county clerk of each county to the comptroller or other officer in the city of St. Louis whose duty it shall be to make up and certify the tax books wherein are ex tended the ad valorem state taxes. It shall be the duty of said clerks and the said comptroller or other proper officer in the city of St. Louis to extend upon the tax books the taxes to be collected and to certify the same to the collectors of the revenue of their respective counties and of the city of St. Louis, who shall collect such taxes at the same time and in the same manner and by the same means as are now or may hereafter be provided by law for the collection of state and county taxes, and to pay the same into the state treasury for the credit of the "Water Pollution Control Bond and Interest Fund."

All funds paid into the Water Pollution Control Bond and Interest Fund shall be and stand appropriated without legislative action to the payment of principal and interest of the said bonds, there to remain until paid out in discharge of the principal of said bonds and the interest accruing thereon, and no part of such fund shall be used for any other purpose so long as any of the principal of said bonds and the interest thereon shall be unpaid.

The General Assembly may enact such laws as may be necessary to carry this amendment into effect.

Section 37(D). Third State Building Bond Issue Authorized—Procedures—Use of Funds

The general assembly may authorize the contracting of an indebtedness on behalf of the state of Missouri and the issuance of bonds or other evidences of indebtedness in the aggregate sum of six hundred million dollars for the purpose of providing funds for improvements of state buildings and property, including state parks, including but not limited to repairing, remodeling, or rebuilding buildings and properties of the state, providing additions thereto or additional buildings where necessary, and for planning, furnishing, equipping and landscaping such improvements and for expenditures for state parks as specified in section 253.040, RSMo, and for grants administered pursuant to sections 204.031, RSMo, 192.600 through 192.620, RSMo, 68.010 to 68.070, RSMo, and 278.080, RSMo, and for construction and improvement of rail and highway access within this state.

The bonds shall be issued by the state board of fund commissioners as necessary to carry on the program of financing, planning, and constructing the improvements specified in this section as determined by the general assembly, provided that the total amount of the bonds authorized hereunder shall be is sued and the same amount appropriated by the general assembly by December 31, 1987. The board of fund commissioners shall offer the bonds at public sale, and shall provide such method as it deems necessary for the advertisement of the sale of each issue of the bonds before they are sold. The proceeds of the sale of the bonds issued hereunder shall be paid into the state treasury and credited to a fund to be designated the "Third State Building Fund" and shall be expended only in the manner provided in this section for the purposes for which the bonds are hereinbefore authorized to be issued. The bonds shall be retired serially and by installments within a period not to exceed twenty-five years from their date of issue and shall bear interest at a rate or rates not exceeding the rate permitted by law. The bonds and the interest thereon shall be paid out of the "Third State Building Bond Interest and Sinking Fund", which is hereby created, and the payment of the bonds and the interest thereon shall be secured by a pledge of the full faith, credit and resources of the state of Missouri. Upon the issuance of the bonds, or any portion thereof, the state board of fund commissioners shall notify the commissioner of administration of the amount of money required, in the remaining portion of the fiscal year during which the bonds are issued, for the payment of interest on the bonds, and of the amount of money required for the payment of interest on the bonds in the next succeeding fiscal year, and to pay the bonds as they mature. Thereafter, within thirty days after the beginning of each fiscal year, the state board of fund commissioners shall notify the commissioner of administration of the amount of money required for the payment of interest on the bonds in the next succeeding fiscal year and to pay the bonds maturing in such next succeeding fiscal year.

The commissioner of administration shall transfer at least monthly from the state revenue fund, after deducting therefrom the proportionate part thereof appropriated for the support of the free public schools, to the credit of the third state building bond interest and sinking fund such sum as may be necessary from time to time until there is transferred to the fund the amount certified to him by the state board of fund commissioners, as hereinbefore provided.

If at any time after the issuance of the bonds it becomes apparent to the commissioner of administration that the funds available in the state revenue fund will not be sufficient for the payment of the third state building bond interest and sinking fund and interest on outstanding obligations of the state, and for the purpose of public education, and the principal and interest maturing on the bonds issued hereunder during the next succeeding fiscal year, a direct tax shall be levied upon all taxable tangible property in the state for the payment of the bonds and the interest that will accrue thereon. in such event, the commissioner of administration shall annually, on or before the first day of July, determine the rate of taxation necessary to be levied upon all taxable tangible property within the state to raise the amount of money needed to pay the principal and interest on such bonds maturing and accruing in the next succeeding fiscal year, taking into consideration available funds, delinquencies and costs of collection. The commissioner of administration shall annually certify the rate of taxation so determined to the county clerk of each county and to the comptroller or other officer in the city of St. Louis whose duty it is to make up and certify the tax books wherein are extended the ad valorem state taxes. The clerks and the comptroller, or other proper officer in the city of St. Louis, shall extend upon the tax books the taxes to be collected and shall certify the same to the collectors of the revenue of their respective counties and of the city of St. Louis, who shall collect such taxes at the same time and in the same manner and by the same means as are now or may hereafter be provided by law for the collection of state and county taxes, and pay the same into the state treasury to the credit of the third state building bond interest and sinking fund.

All funds paid into the third state building bond interest and sinking fund shall be and stand appropriated without legislative action to the payment of principal and interest of the bonds, there to remain until paid out in discharge of the principal of the bonds and the interest accruing thereon, and no part of such fund shall be used for any other purpose so long as any of the principal of the bonds and interest thereon are unpaid. The general assembly may appropriate in any year such amount from the third state building fund as it determines to be necessary for the purposes specified herein. Any amount so appropriated in any year shall be distributed according to the following guidelines:

(1) A minimum of 20% of the total amount of appropriations from the third state building fund in any year shall be used for the repair, replacement and maintenance of state buildings and facilities as determined by the general assembly;

(2) 15% of the total amount of appropriations from the third state building fund in any year shall be allocated for the purpose of stimulating economic development in this state and shall be distributed as follows:

(a) 20% of the appropriations under this subdivision shall be appropriated to the department of highways and transportation for highway purposes;

(b) 20% of the appropriations under this subdivision shall be appropriated to the office of the governor or a department so designated by the governor for transportation purposes other than highways and for capital improvement expenditures as they relate to projects relating to chapter 68, RSMo;

(c) 20% of the appropriations under this subdivision shall be appropriated to fund grants administered pursuant to section 204.031, RSMo;

(d) 26.6% of the appropriations under this subdivision shall be appropriated to fund grants administered pursuant to section 278.080, RSMo;

(e) 13.4% of the appropriations under this subdivision shall be appropriated to fund grants administered pursuant to sections 192.600 through 192.620, RSMo; III § 37(d) 36

(3) A maximum of 65% of the total amount appropriated from the third state building fund in any year shall be distributed among the following departments and agencies of state government as follows:

(a) 2.7% of the appropriations under this subdivision shall be appropriated to the department of agriculture;

(b) .2% of the appropriations under this subdivision shall be appropriated to the department of elementary and secondary education;

(c) 36.3% of the appropriations under this subdivision shall be appropriated to the department of higher education;

(d) 17.0% of the appropriations under this subdivision shall be appropriated to the department of mental health;

(e) 15.1% of the appropriations under this subdivision shall be appropriated to the department of natural resources for state parks and historic preservation;

(f) 1.9% of the appropriations under this subdivision shall be appropriated to the department of public safety;

(g) 18.4% of the appropriations under this subdivision shall be appropriated to the department of corrections and human resources;

(h) 3.4% of the appropriations under this subdivision shall be appropriated to the department of social services;

(i) 5.0% of the appropriations under this subdivision shall be appropriated to the board of public buildings for planning for capital improvement projects to be funded from the third state building fund. The general assembly may enact such laws as may be necessary to carry this amendment into effect. With the exception of those projects involving the repair, replacement or maintenance of state buildings or facilities for which at least 20% of any year's appropriations from the fund are reserved as provided above, no project proposed to be funded from the third state building fund shall be commenced unless the general assembly shall first have specifically authorized such undertaking by passage of legislation apart from its ordinary appropriation process. The additional revenue provided by this section shall not be part of "total state revenue" in sections 17 and 18 of article X of this constitution. The expenditure of this additional revenue shall not be an "expense of state government" under section 20 of article X of this constitution. (Adopted June 8, 1982) Section 37(e). Water pollution control, improvement of drinking water systems and storm water control—bonds authorized, procedure.

1. The general assembly may authorize the contracting of an indebtedness on behalf of the state of Missouri and the issuance of bonds or other evidences of indebtedness not exceeding in the aggregate the sum of two hundred seventy-five million dollars for the purpose of providing funds for use in this state for the control of water pollution and improvements to drinking water systems, including the establishment of water supply hook-ups from unincorporated areas of any county to water supplies, whether or not a particular county as a whole is classified as rural, and for storm water control, through grants and loans administered by the clean water commission and the department of natural resources pursuant to law. The repeal and re-enactment of this section shall not be construed to increase the aggregate amount of indebtedness which may be authorized pursuant to this section above the amount authorized pursuant to this section immediately prior to such repeal and re-enactment. The bonds shall be issued by the state board of fund commissioners from time to time and in such amounts as may be necessary to carry on the program of the clean water commission and the department of natural resources as determined by the general assembly for the financing and constructing of these improvements by any county, municipality, sewer district, water district, or any combination of the same. The board of fund commissioners shall offer such bonds at public sale, and shall provide such method as it may deem necessary for the advertisement of the sale of each issue of bonds before such bonds are sold. The proceeds of the sale or sales of any bonds issued hereunder shall be paid into the state treasury and be credited to a fund to be designated the water pollution control fund. The bonds shall be retired serially and by installments within a period not to exceed twenty-five years from their date of issue and shall bear interest at a rate or rates not exceeding the rate permitted by law. The proceeds of the sale of the bonds herein authorized shall be expended for the purposes for which the bonds are hereinabove authorized to be issued.

2. The bonds and the interest thereon shall be paid out of the "Water Pollution Control Bond and Interest Fund", which is hereby created, and the payment of such bonds and interest thereon shall be secured by a pledge of the full faith, credit and resources of the state of Missouri. Upon the issuance of such bonds, or any portion thereof, the state board of fund commissioners shall notify the commissioner of administration of the amount of money required, in the remaining portion of the fiscal year during which such bonds shall have been issued, for the payment of interest on the bonds, and of the amount of money required for the payment of interest on the bonds in the next succeeding fiscal year, and to pay such bonds as they mature. Thereafter, with in thirty days after the beginning of each fiscal year, the state board of fund commissioners shall notify the commissioner of administration of the amount of money required for the payment of interest on the bonds in the next succeeding fiscal year and to pay such bonds maturing in the next succeeding fiscal year.

3. It shall be the duty of the commissioner of administration to transfer at least monthly, from the state general revenue fund, after deducting therefrom the proportionate part thereof appropriated for the support of the free public schools, and to credit to the water pollution control bond and interest fund such sum as may be necessary from time to time until there shall have been transferred to such fund the amount so certified to the commissioner of administration by the state board of fund commissioners, as provided in this section.

4. If at any time after the issuance of any of the bonds, it shall become apparent to the commissioner of administration that the funds available in the state general revenue fund will not be sufficient for the payment of the sinking fund and interest on outstanding obligations of the state and for the purpose of public education and the principal and interest maturing and accruing on the bonds during the next succeeding fiscal year, a direct tax shall be levied upon all taxable tangible property in the state for the payment of such bonds and the interest that will accrue thereon. in such event, it shall be the duty of the commissioner of administration annually, on or before the first day of July, to determine the rate of taxation necessary to be levied upon all taxable tangible property within the state to raise the amount of money needed to pay the principal of and interest on such bonds maturing and accruing in the next succeeding fiscal year, taking into consideration available funds, delinquencies and costs of collection. The commissioner of administration shall annually certify the rate of taxation so determined to the county clerk of each county to the comptroller or other officer in the city of St. Louis whose duty it shall be to make up and certify the tax books wherein are extended the ad valorem state taxes. It shall be the duty of such clerks and the comptroller or other proper officer in the city of St. Louis to extend upon the tax books the taxes to be collected and to certify the same to the collectors of the revenue of their respective counties and of the city of St. Louis, who shall collect such taxes at the same time and in the same manner and by the means as are now or may hereafter be provided by law for the collection of state and county taxes, and to pay the same into the state treasury for the credit of the water pollution control bond and interest fund.

5. All funds paid into the water pollution control bond and interest fund shall be and stand appropriated without legislative action to the payment of prin cipal and interest of the bonds, there to remain until paid out in discharge of the principal of such bonds and the interest accruing thereon, and no part of such fund shall be used for any other purpose so long as any of the principal of such bonds and the interest thereon shall be unpaid. The general assembly may appropriate in any year such amount from the water pollution control fund as it determines to be necessary for the purposes specified herein. How ever, such appropriations may not exceed fifty million dollars, in the aggregate, for the purpose of providing rural water and sewer grants, including grants for the establishment of water supply hook-ups from unincorporated areas of any county to water supplies, whether or not a particular county as a whole is classified as rural, administered by the department of natural resources pursuant to law, and may not exceed twenty-five million dollars, in the aggregate, for the purpose of storm water control. The general assembly may enact such laws as may be necessary to carry this amendment into effect. (

Section 37(F). Fourth State Building Bond and Interest Fund Created—Bond Issue Authorized, Procedure—Use of Funds

1. The general assembly may authorize the contracting of an indebtedness on behalf of the state of Missouri and the issuance of bonds or other evidences of indebtedness not exceeding in the aggregate the sum of two hundred fifty million dollars for the purpose of providing funds for rebuilding buildings of institutions of higher education including public community colleges, the department of corrections and the division of youth services, providing additions thereto or additional buildings where necessary, for land acquisition, for construction or purchase of buildings, and for planning, furnishing, equipping and landscaping such improvements and buildings. The bonds shall be issued by the state board of fund commissioners from time to time and in such amounts as may be necessary as determined by the general assembly for such purposes. The board of fund commissioners shall offer such bonds at public sale, and shall provide such method as it may deem necessary for the advertisement of the sale of each issue of bonds before such bonds are sold. The proceeds of the sale or sales of any bonds issued under this section shall be paid into the state treasury and be credited to a fund to be designated the fourth state building fund. The bonds shall be retired serially and by installments within a period not to exceed twenty-five years from their date of issue and shall bear interest at a rate or rates not exceeding the rate permitted by law. The proceeds of the sale of the bonds authorized in this section shall be expended for the purposes for which the bonds are authorized to be issued.

2. The bonds and the interest thereon shall be paid out of the "Fourth State Building Bond and Interest Fund", which is hereby created, and the payment of such bonds and the interest thereon shall be secured by a pledge of the full faith, credit and resources of the state of Missouri. Upon the issuance of such bonds, or any portion thereof, the state board of fund commissioners shall notify the commissioner of administration of the amount of money required, in the remaining portion of the fiscal year during which such bonds shall have been issued, for the payment of interest on the bonds, and of the amount of money required for the payment of interest on the bonds in the following fiscal year, and to pay such bonds as they mature. Thereafter, within thirty days after the beginning of each fiscal year, the state board of fund commissioners shall notify the commissioner of administration of the amount of money required for the payment of interest on the bonds in the following fiscal year and to pay such bonds maturing in the following fiscal year.

3. It shall be the duty of the commissioner of administration to transfer at least monthly, from the state general revenue fund or from any other fund established by law for this purpose, after deducting therefrom the proportionate part thereof appropriated for the support of the free public schools, and to credit to the fourth state building bond and interest fund such sum as may be necessary from time to time until there shall have been transferred to such fund the amount so certified to the commissioner of administration by the state board of fund commissioners, as provided in this section.

4. If at any time after the issuance of any of the bonds, it shall become apparent to the commissioner of administration that the funds available in the state general revenue fund will not be sufficient for the payment of the sinking fund and interest on outstanding obligations of the state and for the purpose of public education and the principal and interest maturing and accruing on the bonds during the following fiscal year, a direct tax shall be levied upon all taxable tangible property in the state for the payment of such bonds and the interest that will accrue thereon. in such event, it shall be the duty of the commissioner of administration annually, on or before the first day of July, to determine the rate of taxation necessary to be levied upon all taxable tangible property within the state to raise the amount of money needed to pay the principal of and interest on such bonds maturing and accruing in the following fiscal year, taking into consideration available funds, delinquencies and costs of collection. The commissioner of administration shall annually certify the rate of taxation so determined to the county clerk of each county to the comptroller or other officer in the city of St. Louis whose duty it shall be to make up and certify the tax books wherein are extended the ad valorem state taxes. It shall be the duty of such clerks and the comptroller or other proper officer in the city of St. Louis to extend upon the tax books the taxes to be collected and to certify the same to the collectors of the revenue of their respective counties and of the city of St. Louis, who shall collect such taxes at the same time and in the same manner and by the means as are now or may hereafter be provided by law for the collection of state and county taxes, and to pay the same into the state treasury for the credit of the fourth state building bond and interest fund.

5. All funds paid into the fourth state building bond and interest fund shall be and stand appropriated without legislative action to the payment of principal and interest of the bonds, there to remain until paid out in discharge of the principal of such bonds and the interest accruing thereon, and no part of such fund shall be used for any other purpose so long as any of the principal of such bonds and the interest thereon shall be unpaid. The general assembly may appropriate in any year such amount from the fourth state building fund as it determines to be necessary for the purposes specified in this section. The general assembly may enact such laws as may be necessary to implement the provisions of this section. The additional revenue provided by this section shall not be part of "total state revenue" in sections 17 and 18 of article X of this constitution. The expenditure of such additional revenue shall not be an "expense of state government" under section 20 of article X of this constitution. 6. The governor or his designated representative shall develop in consultation with the state board of fund commissioners a percentage plan for application by African Americans, women and other minority businesses in all state bond programs. The governor or his designated representative shall develop, in consultation with the state board of fund commissioners, a percentage plan for application by African American, women, and other minority, for employment opportunity in the state construction building plan. Such minority business and employment plans shall be filed with the Missouri minority business advocacy commission.

Section 37(G). Rural Water and Sewer Grants and Loans—Bonds Authorized, Procedure

1. in addition to any other indebtedness authorized under this constitution or the laws of this state, the general assembly may authorize the contracting of an indebtedness on behalf of the state of Missouri and the issuance of bonds or other evidences of indebtedness not exceeding in the aggregate the sum of one hundred million dollars for the purpose of providing rural water and sewer grants and loans, including grants for the establishment of water supply hook-ups in unincorporated areas of any county to water supplies, whether or not a particular county as a whole is classified as rural, through grants and loans administered by the clean water commission and the department of natural resources pursuant to procedures in chapter 640, RSMo, and chapter 644, RSMo. The bonds shall be issued by the state board of fund commissioners from time to time and in such amounts as may be necessary to carry on the program of the clean water commission and the department of natural resources as determined by the general assembly for the financing and constructing of these improvements by any county, municipality, sewer district, water district, or any combination of the same. The board of fund commissioners shall offer such bonds at public sale, and shall provide such method as it may deem necessary for the advertisement of the sale of each issue of bonds before such bonds are sold. The proceeds of the sale or sales of any bonds issued hereunder shall be paid into the state treasury and be credited to the water pollution control bond fund. The bonds shall be retired serially and by installments within a period not to exceed twenty-five years from their date of issue and shall bear interest at a rate or rates not exceeding the rate permitted by law. The proceeds of the sale of the bonds herein authorized shall be expended for the purposes for which the bonds are hereinabove authorized to be issued.

2. The bonds and the interest thereon shall be paid out of the water pollution control bond and interest fund and the payment of such bonds and the interest thereon shall be secured by a pledge of the full faith, credit and resources of the state of Missouri. Upon the issuance of such bonds, or any portion thereof, the state board of fund commissioners shall notify the commissioner of administration of the amount of money required, in the remaining portion of the fiscal year during which such bonds shall have been issued, for the payment of interest on the bonds in the next succeeding fiscal year, and to pay such bonds as they mature. Thereafter, within thirty days after the beginning of each fiscal year, the state board of fund commissioners shall notify the commissioner of administration of the amount of money required for the payment of interest on the bonds in the next succeeding fiscal year and to pay such bonds maturing in the next succeeding fiscal year.

3. It shall be the duty of the commissioner of administration to transfer at least monthly, from the state general revenue fund, after deducting therefrom the proportionate part thereof appropriated for the support of the free public schools, and to credit to the water pollution control bond and interest fund such sum as may be necessary from time to time until there shall have been transferred to such fund the amount so certified to the commissioner of administration by the state board of fund commissioners, as provided by this section.

4. If at any time after the issuance of any of the bonds, it shall become apparent to the commissioner of administration that the funds available in the state general revenue fund will not be sufficient for the payment of the sinking fund and interest on outstanding obligations of the state and for the purpose of public education and the principal and interest maturing and accruing on the bonds during the next succeeding fiscal year, a direct tax shall be levied upon all taxable tangible property in the state for the payment of such bonds and the interest that will accrue thereon. in such event, it shall be the duty of the commissioner of administration annually, on or before the first day of July, to determine the rate of taxation necessary to be levied upon all taxable tangible property within the state to raise the amount of money needed to pay the principal of and interest on such bonds maturing and accruing in the next succeeding fiscal year, taking into consideration available funds, delinquencies and costs of collection. The commissioner of administration shall annually certify the rate of taxation so determined to the county clerk of each county and to the comptroller or other officer in the city of St. Louis whose duty it shall be to make up and certify the tax books wherein are extended the ad valorem state taxes. It shall be the duty of such clerks and the comptroller or other proper officer in the city of St. Louis to extend upon the tax books the taxes to be collected and to certify the same to the collectors of the revenue of their respective counties and of the city of St. Louis, who shall collect such taxes at the same time and in the same manner and by the means as are now or may hereafter be provided by law for the collection of state and county taxes, and to pay the same into the state treasury for the credit of the water pollution control bond and interest fund.

5. All funds paid into the water pollution control bond and interest fund shall be and stand appropriated without legislative action to the payment of principal and interest of the bonds, there to remain until paid out in discharge of the principal of such bonds and the interest accruing thereon, and no part of such fund shall be used for any other purpose so long as any of the principal of such bonds and the interest thereon shall be unpaid. The general assembly may appropriate in any year such amount from the water pollution control fund as it determines to be necessary for the purposes specified herein. However, such appropriations may not exceed ten million dollars for the purpose of providing rural water and sewer grants and loans, including grants for the establishment of water supply hook-ups from unincorporated areas of any county to water supplies, whether or not a particular county as a whole is classified as rural, administered by the department of natural resources pursuant to law. The general assembly may enact such laws as may be necessary to carry this amendment into effect.

Section 37(H). Stormwater Control—Bonds Authorized, Procedure

1. in addition to any other indebtedness authorized under this constitution or the laws of this state, the general assembly may authorize the contracting of an indebtedness on behalf of the state of Missouri and the issuance of bonds or other evidences of indebtedness not exceeding in the aggregate the sum of two hundred million dollars for the purpose of providing funds for use in this state for stormwater control plans, studies and projects in counties of the first classification and in any city not within a county, through grants and loans administered by the clean water commission and the department of natural resources pursuant to the procedures in chapter 644, RSMo. The bonds shall be issued by the state board of fund commissioners from time to time and in such amounts as may be necessary to carry on the program of the clean water commission and the department of natural resources as determined by the general assembly for the financing and constructing of these plans, studies and projects by any municipality, public sewer district, sewer district established pursuant to article VI, section 30(a) of the Missouri Constitution, public water district, or any combination of the same located in a county of the first classification or in any city not within a county or by any county of the first classification. The board of fund commissioners shall offer such bonds at public sale, and shall provide such method as it may deem necessary for the advertisement of the sale of each issue of bonds before such bonds are sold. The proceeds of the sale or sales of any bonds issued hereunder shall be paid into the state treasury and be credited to a fund to be designated the "Stormwater Control Fund". The bonds shall be retired serially and by installments within a period not to exceed twenty-five years from their date of issue and shall bear interest at a rate or rates not exceeding the rate permitted by law. The proceeds of the sale of the bonds herein authorized shall be expended for the purposes for which the bonds are hereinabove authorized to be issued.

2. The bonds and the interest thereon shall be paid out of the "Stormwater Control Bond and Interest Fund", which is hereby created, and the payment of such bonds and the interest thereon shall be secured by a pledge of the full faith, credit and resources of the state of Missouri. Upon the issuance of such bonds, or any portion thereof, the state board of fund commissioners shall notify the commissioner of administration of the amount of money required, in the remaining portion of the fiscal year during which such bonds shall have been issued, for the payment of interest on the bonds, and of the amount of money required for the payment of interest on the bonds in the next succeeding fiscal year, and to pay such bonds as they mature. Thereafter, within thirty days after the beginning of each fiscal year, the state board of fund commissioners shall notify the commissioner of administration of the amount of money required for the payment of interest on the bonds in the next succeeding fiscal year and to pay such bonds maturing in the next succeeding fiscal year.

3. It shall be the duty of the commissioner of administration to transfer at least monthly, from the state general revenue fund, after deducting therefrom the proportionate part thereof appropriated for the support of the free public schools, and to credit to the stormwater control bond and interest fund such sum as may be necessary from time to time until there shall have been transferred to such fund the amount so certified to the commissioner of administration by the state board of fund commissioners, as provided in this section.

4. If at any time after the issuance of any of the bonds, it shall become apparent to the commissioner of administration that the funds available in the state general revenue fund will not be sufficient for the payment of the sinking fund and interest on outstanding obligations of the state and for the purpose of public education and the principal and interest maturing and accruing on the bonds during the next succeeding fiscal year, a direct tax shall be levied upon all taxable tangible property in the state for the payment of such bonds and the interest that will accrue thereon. in such event, it shall be the duty of the commissioner of administration annually, on or before the first day of July, to determine the rate of taxation necessary to be levied upon all taxable tangible property within the state to raise the amount of money needed to pay the principal of and interest on such bonds maturing and accruing in the next succeeding fiscal year, taking into consideration available funds, delinquencies and costs of collection. The commissioner of administration shall annually certify the rate of taxation so determined to the county clerk of each county and to the comptroller or other officer in the city of St. Louis whose duty it shall be to make up and certify the tax books wherein are extended the ad valorem state taxes. It shall be the duty of such clerks and the comptroller or other proper officer in the city of St Louis to extend upon the tax books the taxes to be collected and to certify the same to the collectors of the revenue of their respective counties and of the city of St.

Louis, who shall collect such taxes at the same time and in the same manner and by the means as are now or may hereafter be provided by law for the collection of state and county taxes, and to pay the same into the state treasury for the credit of the stormwater control bond and interest fund.

5. All funds paid into the stormwater control bond and interest fund shall be and stand appropriated without legislative action to the payment of principal and interest of the bonds, there to remain until paid out in discharge of the principal of such bonds and the interest accruing thereon, and no part of such fund shall be used for any other purpose so long as any of the principal of such bonds and the interest thereon shall be unpaid. The general assembly may appropriate in any year such amount from the stormwater control fund as it determines to be necessary for the purposes specified in this section. Grants may be combined with loans such as those provided by the commission or the department. Funding for grants or loans from the stormwater control fund shall be initially offered to eligible recipients in counties of the first classification and in a city not within a county in an amount equal to the percentage ratio that the population of the recipient county or city bears to the total population of all counties of the first classification and cities not within a county as determined by the last decennial census. Any city with a population of at least twenty-five thousand inhabitants located in such counties of the first classification shall initially be offered such funds in an amount equal to the percentage ratio that the city's population bears to the total population of the county. Other provisions of this section notwithstanding, in those cities or counties served by a sewer district established pursuant to article VI, section 30(a) of the Missouri Constitution, such district shall receive the grants or loans directly. Any funds not accepted in the initial offers of funding under this subsection shall be subsequently offered to recipients of the initial offer of funding who continue to have eligible projects until all funds have been accepted. Any such subsequent funding offer shall be equal to the percentage ratio that the population of the funding recipient bears to the total population of all other recipients with eligible projects.

6. Repayments of storm water loans and any interest payments on such loans shall be deposited in a fund as provided by law for the purposes of financing and constructing storm water control plans, studies, and projects. Any unexpended balance in such fund shall not be subject to biennial transfer under the provisions of section 33.080, RSMo, and all interest earned shall accrue to the fund. 7. The general assembly may enact such laws as may be necessary to carry out the provisions of this section.

Section 38(A). Limitation On Use of State Funds and Credit—Exceptions—Public Calamity—Blind Pensions—Old Age Assistance—Aid to Children—Direct Relief— Adjusted Compensation for Veterans—Rehabilitation— Participation in Federal Aid

The general assembly shall have no power to grant public money or property, or lend or authorize the lending of public credit, to any private person, association or corporation, excepting aid in public calamity, and general laws providing for pensions for the blind, for old age assistance, for aid to dependent or crippled children or the blind, for direct relief, for adjusted compensation, bonus or rehabilitation for discharged members of the armed services of the United States who were bonafide residents of this state during their service, and for the rehabilitation of other persons. Money or property may also be received from the United States and be redistributed together with public money of this state for any public purpose designated by the United States.

Section 38(B). Tax Levy for Blind Pension Fund

The general assembly shall provide an annual tax of not less than one-half of one cent nor more than three cents on the one hundred dollars valuation of all taxable property to be levied and collected as other taxes, for the purpose of providing a fund to be appropriated and used for the pensioning of the deserving blind as provided by law. Any balance remaining in the fund after the payment of the pensions may be appropriated for the adequate support of the commission for the blind, and any remaining balance shall be transferred to the distributive public school fund.

Section 38(C). Neighborhood Improvement Districts, Cities and Counties May be Authorized to Establish, Powers and Duties—Limitation On Indebtedness

1. The general assembly may authorize cities and counties to create neighborhood improvement districts and incur indebtedness and issue general obligation bonds to pay for all or part of the cost of public improvements with in such districts. The cost of all indebtedness so incurred shall be levied and assessed by the governing body of the city or county on the property benefited by such improvements. The city or county shall collect the special assessments so levied and use the same to reimburse the city or county for the amount paid or to be paid by it on the general obligation bonds issued for such improvements.

2. Neighborhood improvement districts may be created by a city or county only when approved by the vote of a percentage of electors voting thereon within such district, or by a petition signed by the owners of record of a percentage of real property located within such district, that is equal to the percentage of voter approval required for the issuance of general obligation bonds under article VI, section 26.

3. The total amount of city or county indebtedness for all such districts shall not exceed ten percent of the assessed valuation of all taxable tangible property, as shown by the last completed property assessment for state or local purposes, within the city or county.

Section 38(D). Stem Cell Research—Title of Law—Permissible Research—Violations, Penalty—Report Required, When—Prohibited Acts—Definitions

1. This section shall be known as the "Missouri Stem Cell Research and Cures Initiative."

2. to ensure that Missouri patients have access to stem cell therapies and cures, that Missouri researchers can conduct stem cell research in the state, and that all such research is conducted safely and ethically, any stem cell research permitted under federal law may be conducted in Missouri, and any stem cell therapies and cures permitted under federal law may be provided to patients in Missouri, subject to the requirements of federal law and only the following additional limitations and requirements:

(1) No person may clone or attempt to clone a human being.

(2) No human blastocyst may be produced by fertilization solely for the purpose of stem cell research.

(3) No stem cells may be taken from a human blastocyst more than fourteen days after cell division begins; provided, however, that time during which a blastocyst is frozen does not count against the fourteen- day limit.

(4) No person may, for valuable consideration, purchase or sell human blastocysts or eggs for stem cell research or stem cell therapies and cures.

(5) Human blastocysts and eggs obtained for stem cell research or stem cell therapies and cures must have been donated with voluntary and informed consent, documented in writing.

(6) Human embryonic stem cell research may be conducted only by persons that, within 180 days of the effective date of this section or otherwise prior to commencement of such research, whichever is later, have

(a) provided oversight responsibility and approval authority for such research to an embryonic stem cell research oversight committee whose membership includes representatives of the public and medical and scientific experts;

(b) adopted ethical standards for such research that comply with the requirements of this section; and

(c) obtained a determination from an Institutional Review Board that the research complies with all applicable federal statutes and regulations that the Institutional Review Board is responsible for administering.

(7) All stem cell research and all stem cell therapies and cures must be conducted and provided in accordance with state and local laws of general applicability, including but not limited to laws concerning scientific and medical practices and patient safety and privacy, to the extent that any such laws do not

(i) prevent, restrict, obstruct, or discourage any stem cell research or stem cell therapies and cures that are permitted by the provisions of this section other than this subdivision (7) to be conducted or provided, or

(ii) create disincentives for any person to engage in or otherwise associate with such research or therapies and cures.

3. Any person who knowingly and willfully violates in this state subdivision (1) of subsection 2 of this section commits a crime and shall be punished by imprisonment for a period of up to fifteen years or by the imposition of a fine of up to two hundred fifty thousand dollars, or by both. Any person who knowingly and willfully violates in this state subdivisions (2) or (3) of subsection 2 of this section commits a crime and shall be punished by imprisonment for a period of up to ten years or by the imposition of a fine of up to one hundred thousand dollars, or by both. A civil action may be brought against any person who knowingly and willfully violates in this state any of subdivisions (1) through

(6) of subsection 2 of this section, and the state in such action shall be entitled to a judgment recovering a civil penalty of up to fifty thousand dollars per violation, requiring disgorgement of any financial profit derived from such violation, and/or enjoining any further such violation. The attorney general shall have the exclusive right to bring a civil action for such violation. Venue for such action shall be the county in which the alleged violation occurred.

4. Each institution, hospital, other entity, or other person conducting human embryonic stem cell research in the state shall

(i) prepare an annual report stating the nature of the human embryonic stem cells used in, and the purpose of, the research conducted during the prior calendar year, and certifying compliance with subdivision (6) of subsection 2 of this section; and

(ii) no later than June 30 of the subsequent year, make such report available to the public and inform the Secretary of State how the public may obtain copies of or otherwise gain access to the report. The report shall not contain private or confidential medical, scientific, or other information. Individuals conducting research at an institution, hospital, or other entity that prepares and makes available a report pursuant to this subsection 4 concerning such research are not required to prepare and make available a separate report concerning that same research. A civil action may be brought against any institution, hospital, other entity, or other person that fails to prepare or make available the report or inform the Secretary of State how the public may obtain copies of or otherwise gain access to the report, and the state in such action shall be entitled as its sole remedy to an affirmative injunction requiring such institution, hospital, other entity, or other person to prepare and make available the report or inform the Secretary of State how the public may obtain or otherwise gain access to the report. The attorney general shall have the exclusive right to bring a civil action for such violation.

5. to ensure that no governmental body or official arbitrarily restricts funds designated for purposes other than stem cell research or stem cell therapies and cures as a means of inhibiting lawful stem cell research or stem cell therapies and cures, no state or local governmental body or official shall eliminate, reduce, deny, or withhold any public funds provided or eligible to be provided to a person that

(i) lawfully conducts stem cell research or provides stem cell therapies and cures, allows for such research or therapies and cures to be conducted or provided on its premises, or is otherwise associated with such research or therapies and cures, but

(ii) receives or is eligible to receive such public funds for purposes other than such stem cell-related activities, on account of, or otherwise for the purpose of creating disincentives for any person to engage in or otherwise associate with, or preventing, restricting, obstructing, or discouraging, such stem cell-related activities. 6. As used in this section, the following terms have the following meanings:

(1) "Blastocyst" means a small mass of cells that results from cell division, caused either by fertilization or somatic cell nuclear transfer, that has not been implanted in a uterus.

(2) "Clone or attempt to clone a human being" means to implant in a uterus or attempt to implant in a uterus anything other than the product of fertilization of an egg of a human female by a sperm of a human male for the purpose of initiating a pregnancy that could result in the creation of a human fetus, or the birth of a human being.

(3) "Donated" means donated for use in connection either with scientific or medical research or with medical treatment.

(4) "Fertilization" means the process whereby an egg of a human female and the sperm of a human male form a zygote (i.e., fertilized egg).

(5) "Human embryonic stem cell research," also referred to as "early stem cell research," means any scientific or medical research involving human stem cells derived from in vitro fertilization blastocysts or from somatic cell nuclear transfer. for purposes of this section, human embryonic stem cell research does not include stem cell clinical trials.

(6) "in vitro fertilization" means fertilization of an egg with a sperm outside the body.

(7) "Institutional Review Board" means a specially constituted review board established and operating in accordance with federal law as set forth in 42 U.S.C. 289, 45 C.F.R. Part 46, and any other applicable federal statutes and regulations, as amended from time to time.

(8) "Permitted under federal law" means, as it relates to stem cell research and stem cell therapies and cures, any such research, therapies, and cures that are not prohibited under federal law from being conducted or provided, regardless of whether federal funds are made available for such activities.

(9) "Person" means any natural person, corporation, association, partnership, public or private institution, or other legal entity.

(10) "Private or confidential medical, scientific, or other information" means any private or confidential patient, medical, or personnel records or matters, intellectual property or work product, whether patentable or not and including but not limited to any scientific or technological innovations in which an entity or person involved in the research has a proprietary interest, per-publication scientific working papers, research, or data, and any other matter excepted from disclosure under Chapter 610, RSMo, as amended from time to time.

(11) "Solely for the purpose of stem cell research" means producing human blastocysts using in vitro fertilization exclusively for stem cell research, but does not include producing any number of human blastocysts for the purpose of treating human infertility.

(12) "Sperm" means mature spermatozoa or precursor cells such as spermatids and spermatocytes.

(13) "Stem cell" means a cell that can divide multiple times and give rise to specialized cells in the body, and includes but is not limited to the stem cells generally referred to as

(i) adult stem cells that are found in some body tissues (including but not limited to adult stem cells derived from adult body tissues and from discarded umbilical cords and placentas), and

(ii) embryonic stem cells (including but not limited to stem cells derived from in vitro fertilization blastocysts and from cell reprogramming techniques such as somatic cell nuclear transfer).

(14) "Stem cell clinical trials" means federally regulated clinical trials involving stem cells and human subjects designed to develop, or assess or test the efficacy or safety of, medical treatments.

(15) "Stem cell research" means any scientific or medical research involving stem cells. for purposes of this section, stem cell research does not include stem cell clinical trials.

(16) "Stem cell therapies and cures" means any medical treatment that involves or otherwise derives from the use of stem cells, and that is used to treat or cure any disease or injury. for purposes of this section, stem cell therapies and cures does include stem cell clinical trials.

(17) "Valuable consideration" means financial gain or advantage, but does not include reimbursement for reasonable costs incurred in connection with the removal, processing, disposal, preservation, quality control, storage, transfer, or donation of human eggs, sperm, or blastocysts, including lost wages of the donor. Valuable consideration also does not include the consideration paid to a donor of human eggs or sperm by a fertilization clinic or sperm bank, as well as any other consideration expressly allowed by federal law.

7. The provisions of this section and of all state and local laws, regulations, rules, charters, ordinances, and other governmental actions shall be construed in favor of the conduct of stem cell research and the provision of stem cell therapies and cures. No state or local law, regulation, rule, charter, ordinance, or other governmental action shall

(i) prevent, restrict, obstruct, or discourage any stem cell research or stem cell therapies and cures that are permitted by this section to be conducted or provided, or

(ii) create disincentives for any person to engage in or otherwise associate with such research or therapies and cures. 8. The provisions of this section are self-executing. All of the provisions of this section are severable. If any provision of this section is found by a court of competent jurisdiction to be unconstitutional or unconstitutionally enacted, the remaining provisions of this section shall be and remain valid.

Section 39. Limitation of Power of General Assembly

The general assembly shall not have power:

(1) to give or lend or to authorize the giving or lending of the credit of the state in aid or to any person, association, municipal or other corporation;

(2) to pledge the credit of the state for the payment of the liabilities, present or prospective, of any individual, association, municipal or other corporation;

(3) to grant or to authorize any county or municipal authority to grant any extra compensation, fee or allowance to a public officer, agent, servant or contractor after service has been rendered or a contract has been entered into and performed in whole or in part;

(4) to pay or to authorize the payment of any claim against the state or any county or municipal corporation of the state under any agreement or contract made without express authority of law;

(5) to release or extinguish or to authorize the releasing or extinguishing, in whole or in part, without consideration, the indebtedness, liability or obligation of any corporation or individual due this state or any county or municipal corporation;

(6) to make any appropriation of money for the payment, or on account of or in recognition of any claims audited or that may hereafter be audited by virtue of an act entitled "An Act to Audit and Adjust the War Debts of the State," approved March 19, 1874, or any act of a similar nature, until the claim so audited shall have been presented to and paid by the government of the United States to this state;

(7) to act, when convened in extra session by the governor, upon subjects other than those specially designated in the proclamation calling said session or recommended by special message to the general assembly after the convening of an extra session;

(8) to remove the seat of government from the City of Jefferson;

(9) Except as otherwise provided in section 39(b), section 39(c), section 39(e) or section 39(f) of this article, to authorize lotteries or gift enterprises for any purpose, and shall enact laws to prohibit the sale of lottery or gift enterprise tickets, or tickets in any scheme in the nature of a lottery; except that, nothing in this section shall be so construed as to prevent or prohibit citizens of this state from participating in games or contests of skill or chance where no consideration is required to be given for the privilege or opportunity of participating or for receiving the award or prize and the term "lottery or gift enterprise" shall mean only those games or contests whereby money or something of value is ex changed directly for the ticket or chance to participate in the game or contest. The general assembly may, by law, provide standards and conditions to regulate or guarantee the awarding of prizes provided for in such games or con tests under the provision of this subdivision;

(10) to impose a use or sales tax upon the use, purchase or acquisition of property paid for out of the funds of any county or other political subdivision.

Section 39(A). Bingo May be Authorized—Requirements

The game commonly known as bingo when conducted by religious, charitable, fraternal, veteran or service organizations is not a lottery or gift enterprise within the meaning of subdivision (9) of section 39 of this article if the general assembly authorizes by law that religious, charitable, fraternal, service, or veteran organizations may conduct the game commonly known as bingo, upon the pay ment of the license fee and the issuance of the license as provided for by law. Any such law shall include the following requirements:

(1) All net receipts over and above the actual cost of conducting the game as set by law shall be used only for charitable, religious or philanthropic purposes, and no receipts shall be used to compensate in any manner any person who works for or is in any way affiliated with the licensed organization;

(2) No license shall be granted to any organization unless it has been in continuous existence for at least five years immediately prior to the application for the license. An organization must have twenty bonafide members to be considered to be in existence;

(3) No person shall participate in the management, conduct or operation of any game unless that person:

(a) Has been a bonafide member of the licensed organization for the two years immediately preceding such participation, and volunteers the time and service necessary to conduct the game;

(b) Is not a paid staff person for the licensed organization;

(c) Is not and has never been a professional gambler or gambling promoter;

(d) Has never purchased a tax stamp for wagering or gambling activity;

(e) Has never been convicted of any felony;

(f) Has never been convicted of or pleaded nolo contendere to any illegal gambling activity;

(g) Is of good moral character;

(4) Any person, any officer or director of any firm or corporation, and any partner of any partnership renting or leasing to a licensed organization any equip ment or premises for use in a game shall meet all of the qualifications of paragraph (3) except subparagraph (a);

(5) No lease, rental arrangement or purchase arrangement for any equipment or premise for use in a game shall provide for payment in excess of the reasonable market rental rate for such premises and in no case shall any payment based on a percentage of the gross receipts or proceeds be permitted;

(6) No person, firm, partnership or corporation shall receive any remuneration or profit for participating in the management, conduct or operation of the game;

(7) No advertising of any game shall be permitted except on the premises of the licensed organization or through ordinary communications between the organization and its members;

(8) Any other requirement the general assembly finds necessary to insure that any games are conducted solely for the benefit of the eligible organizations and the general community.

STATE LOTTERY

Section 39(B). State Lottery, Authority to Establish—Lottery Proceeds Fund Established, Purpose

1. The general assembly shall have authority to authorize a Missouri state lottery by law. If such legislation is adopted, there shall be created a "State Lottery Com mission" consisting of five members who shall be appointed by the governor with the advice and consent of the senate and who may be removed, for cause by the governor and who shall be chosen from the state at large and represent a broad geographic spectrum with no more than one member chosen from each federal congressional district. Each member at the time of his appointment and qualification shall have been a resident of this state for a period of at least five years next preceding his appointment and qualification and shall also be a qualified elector therein and be not less than thirty years of age. No more than three members of the commission shall be members of the same political party. Members of the commission shall have three-year terms as provided by law. Members of the commission shall receive no salary but shall receive their actual expenses incurred in the performance of their responsibilities. The commission

2. The money received by the Missouri state lottery commission from the sale of Missouri lottery tickets, and from all other sources, shall be deposited in the "State Lottery Fund", which is hereby created in the state treasury.

3. The monies received from the Missouri state lottery shall be governed by appropriation of the general assembly. Beginning July 1, 1993, monies representing net proceeds after payment of prizes and administrative expenses shall be transferred by appropriation to the "Lottery Proceeds Fund" which is hereby created within the state treasury and such monies in the lottery proceeds fund shall be appropriated solely for public institutions of elementary, secondary and higher education.

4. A minimum of forty-five percent of the money received from the sale of Missouri state lottery tickets shall be awarded as prizes.

5. The commission shall have the authority to purchase and hold title to any securities of the United States government or its agencies and instrumentalities thereof for prizes, as provided by law.

6. Until July 1, 1993, any person possessing a department of revenue retail sales license as provided by law or any chartered civic, fraternal, charitable or political organization or labor organization shall be eligible to obtain a license to act as a lottery ticket sales agent except a license to act as an agent to sell lottery tickets shall not be issued to any person primarily engaged in business as a lottery ticket sales agent. Until July 1, 1993, the general assembly may impose additional qualifications on such persons to obtain a lottery ticket sales agent license as it deems appropriate. Until July 1, 1993, the commission is also authorized to sell lottery tickets at its office and at special events as provided by law. Beginning July 1, 1993, the general assembly shall enact laws governing lottery ticket sales.

7. Revenues produced from the conduct of a state lottery shall not be part of "total state revenues" as defined in sections 17 and 18 of article X of this constitution and the expenditure of such revenue shall not be an "expense of state government" under section 20 of article X of this constitution.

Section 39(C). Parimutuel Wagering May be Authorized by General Assembly—Horse Racing Commission Established, Election Procedure to Adopt Or Reject Horse Racing

1. The general assembly may authorize on track parimutuel betting on horse racing in a manner provided by law. There is hereby created the Missouri Horse Racing Commission which shall consist of five members appointed by the governor with the advice and consent of the senate. Members of the commission shall be citizens and eligible voters of Missouri and shall not have been convicted of a felony. Not more than three members shall be affiliated with the same political party, and not more than one member may be a resident of any one congressional district or of any single county or of the City of St. Louis. of the members first appointed, one shall be appointed for a one year term, one shall be appointed for a two year term, one shall be appointed for a three year term, one shall be appointed for a four year term and one shall be appointed for a five year term; and thereafter members shall be appointed for terms of five years. The governor shall designate one of the members to be chairman. The governor may remove any member of the commission from office for malfeasance or neglect of duty in office. Members of the commission shall be reimbursed and paid for the expenses which they reasonably incur in the performance of their official duties, but they shall not, however, be paid a salary or other remuneration for their services unless such be authorized by law. No person may serve as a member of the commission and his office shall be deemed vacated if:

(i) The member, the member's spouse, child or parent owns any interest in a race track licensed by the Commission.

(ii) The member, the member's spouse, child or parent is an officer, em ploy ee, consultant or otherwise receives any remuneration from race track licensee.

(iii) The member, the member's spouse, child or parent holds a financial interest in a management or concession contract with a race track licensee. A member shall not, however, be disqualified because either the member or the member's spouse, child or parent is a horse owner or a horse breeder whose horse participates as other horses and wins purses or awards in a race at a licensed race track.

2. At the general election to be held in November, 1986, every officer or body in charge of the elections shall order the following question on the ballot: "Shall parimutuel wagering upon horse races be permitted in .... County (or the City of St. Louis)?" This question may also be ordered upon the ballot at the general election occurring in 1988 and every four years thereafter by the governing body of any county where parimutuel wagering has not been previously authorized. The general provisions of law with respect to the conduct of elections and the submission of questions to voters for determination shall apply insofar as they are applicable. No license shall be issued by the commission authorizing parimutuel wagering within the grounds or enclosure of a racetrack until a majority of the qualified voters of the county where the race track is proposed to be located vote to accept parimutuel wagering in that county at one of the elections referred to above.

Once parimutuel wagering on horse racing has been accepted by the voters of that county at an appropriate election, no other vote shall be held on the question of the legality of such wagering in that county. If the qualified voters of the county reject parimutuel wagering on horse races in that county, no elections shall be held on the question in that county except as in the manner specified above. As used in this section, the term "county" includes the City of St. Louis.

Section 39(D). Gaming Revenues to be Appropriated to Public Institutions of Elementary, Secondary and Higher Education

All state revenues derived from the conduct of all gaming activities as are now or hereafter authorized by this constitution or by law, unless otherwise provided by law on the effective date of this section, shall be appropriated beginning July 1, 1993, solely for the public institutions of elementary, secondary and higher education and shall not be included within the definition of "total state revenues" in section 17 of article X of this constitution.

Section 39(E). Riverboat Gambling Authorized On Missouri and Mississippi Rivers—Boats in Moats Authorized

The general assembly is authorized to permit upon the Mississippi and Missouri Rivers only, which shall include artificial spaces that contain water and that are within 1000 feet of the closest edge of the main channel of either of those rivers, lotteries, gift enterprises and games of chance to be conducted on excursion gambling boats and floating facilities. Any license issued before or after the adoption date of this amendment for any excursion gambling boat or floating facility located in any such artificial space shall be deemed to be authorized by the General Assembly and to be in compliance with this Section.

NOTICE: You are advised that the proposed constitutional amendment may be construed to change, repeal, or modify by implication Article III, Sections 39, 39(9), and 39(e). (Adopted November 8, 1994) (Amended November 3, 1998) Section 39(f).

Raffles and Sweepstakes Authorized

Any organization recognized as charitable or religious pursuant to federal law may sponsor raffles and sweepstakes in which a person risks something of value for a prize. The general assembly may, by law, provide standards and conditions to regulate or guarantee the awarding of prizes provided for in such raffles or sweepstakes.

Section 40. Limitations On Passage of Local and Special Laws

The general assembly shall not pass any local or special law:

(1) authorizing the creation, extension or impairment of liens;

(2) granting divorces;

(3) changing the venue in civil or criminal cases;

(4) regulating the practice or jurisdiction of, or changing the rules of evidence in any judicial proceeding or inquiry before courts, sheriffs, commissioners, arbitrators or other tribunals, or providing or changing methods for the collection of debts, or the enforcing of judgments, or prescribing the effect of judicial sales of real estate;

(5) summoning or empaneling grand or petit juries;

(6) for limitation of civil actions;

(7) remitting fines, penalties and forfeitures or refunding money legally paid into the treasury;

(8) extending the time for the assessment or collection of taxes, or otherwise relieving any assessor or collector of taxes from the due performance of their duties, or their securities from liability;

(9) changing the law of descent or succession;

(10) giving effect to informal or invalid wills or deeds;

(11) affecting the estates of minors or persons under disability;

(12) authorizing the adoption or legitimation of children;

(13) declaring any named person of age;

(14) changing the names of persons or places;

(15) vacating town plats, roads, streets or alleys;

(16) relating to cemeteries, graveyards or public grounds not of the state;

(17) authorizing the laying out, opening, altering or maintaining roads, highways, streets or alleys;

(18) for opening and conducting elections, or fixing or changing the place of voting;

(19) locating or changing county seats;

(20) creating new townships or changing the boundaries of townships or school districts;

(21) creating offices, prescribing the powers and duties of officers in, or regulating the affairs of counties, cities, townships, election or school districts;

(22) incorporating cities, towns, or villages or changing their charters;

(23) regulating the fees or extending the powers of aldermen, magistrates or constables;

(24) regulating the management of public schools, the building or repairing of schoolhouses, and the raising of money for such purposes;

(25) legalizing the unauthorized or invalid acts of any officer or agent of the state or of any county or municipality;

(26) fixing the rate of interest;

(27) regulating labor, trade, mining or manufacturing;

(28) granting to any corporation, association or individual any special or exclusive right, privilege or immunity, or to any corporation, association or individual the right to lay down a railroad track;

(29) relating to ferries or bridges, except for the erection of bridges crossing streams which form the boundary between this and any other state;

(30) where a general law can be made applicable, and whether a general law could have been made applicable is a judicial question to be judicially determined without regard to any legislative assertion on that subject.

Section 41. Indirect Enactment of Local and Special Laws —Repeal of Local and Special Laws

The general assembly shall not indirectly enact a special or local law by the partial repeal of a general law; but laws repealing local or special acts may be passed.

Section 42. Notice of Proposed Local Or Special Laws

No local or special law shall be passed unless a notice, setting forth the intention to apply therefor and the substance of the contemplated law, shall have been published in the locality where the matter or thing to be affected is situated at least thirty days prior to the introduction of the bill into the general assembly and in the manner provided by law. Proof of publication shall be filed with the general assembly before the act shall be passed and the notice shall be recited in the act.

Section 43. Title and Control of Lands of United States—Exemption From Taxation—Taxation of Lands of Nonresidents

The general assembly shall never interfere with the primary disposal of the soil by the United States, nor with any regulation which Congress may find necessary for securing the title in such soil to bona fide purchasers. No tax shall be imposed on lands the property of the United States; nor shall lands belonging to persons residing without the state ever be taxed at a higher rate than lands belonging to persons residing within the state.

Section 44. Uniform Interest Rates

No law shall be valid fixing rates of interest or return for the loan or use of money, or the service or other charges made or imposed in connection therewith, for any particular group or class engaged in lending money. The rates of interest fixed by law shall be applicable generally and to all lenders without regard to the type or classification of their business.

Section 45. Congressional Apportionment

When the number of representatives to which the state is entitled in the House of the Congress of the United States under the census of 1950 and each census thereafter is certified to the governor, the general assembly shall by law divide the state into districts corresponding with the number of representatives to which it is entitled, which districts shall be composed of contiguous territory as compact and as nearly equal in population as may be.

Section 45(A). Term Limitations for Members of U.S. Congress—Effective When—Voluntary Observance Required, When

(1) No United States Senator from Missouri shall serve more than two terms in the United States Senate, and no United States Representative from Missouri shall serve more than four terms in the United States House of Representatives. This limitation on the number of terms shall apply to terms of office beginning on or after the effective date of this section. Any person appointed or elected to fill a vacancy in the United States Congress and who serves at least one-half of a term of office shall be considered to have served a term in that office for purposes of this subsection (1). The provisions of this subsection (1) shall become effective whenever at least one-half of the states enact term limits for their members of the United States Congress.

(2) The people of Missouri declare that the provisions of this section shall be deemed severable and that their intention is that federal officials elected from Missouri will continue voluntarily to observe the wishes of the people as stated in this section in the event any provision thereof is held invalid.

Section 46. Militia

The general assembly shall provide for the organization, equipment, regulations and functions of an adequate militia, and shall conform the same as nearly as practicable to the regulations for the government of the armed forces of the United States.

Section 46(A). Emergency Duties and Powers of Assembly On Enemy Attack

The General Assembly, in order to ensure continuity of state and local governmental operations in periods of emergency only resulting from disasters occurring in this state caused by enemy attack on the United States, shall have the power to such extent as the General Assembly deems advisable. in the event there occurs in this state a disaster caused by enemy attack on the United States, the General Assembly shall immediately convene in the City of Jefferson or in such place as designated by joint proclamation of the highest presiding officers of each house, and shall have power

(1) to provide by legislative enactment for prompt and temporary succession to the powers and duties of public offices, of whatever nature and whether filled by election or appointment, the incumbents of which may become unavailable for carrying on the powers and duties of such offices, and

(2) to adopt by legislative enactment such other legislation as may be necessary and proper for insuring the continuity of governmental operations. Not with standing the power conferred by this section of the constitution, elections shall always be called as soon as possible to fill any elective vacancies in any office temporarily occupied by operation of any legislation enacted pursuant to the provisions of this section.

Section 47. State Parks—Appropriations for, Required

for twelve years beginning with the year 1961, the general assembly shall appropriate for each year out of the general revenue fund, an amount not less than that produced annually at a tax rate of one cent on each one hundred dollars assessed valuation of the real and tangible personal property taxable by the state, for the exclusive purpose of providing a state park fund to be expended and used by the agency authorized by law to control and supervise state parks, and historic sites of the state, for the purposes of the acquisition, supervision, operation, maintenance, development, control, regulation and restoration of state parks and state park property, as may be determined by such agency; and thereafter the general assembly shall appropriate such amounts as may be reasonably necessary for such purposes.

The amount required to be appropriated by this section may be reduced to meet budgetary demands provided said appropriation is not less than that appropriated for the prior similar appropriation period.

Section 48. Historical Memorials and Monuments—Acquisition of Property

The general assembly may enact laws and make appropriations to preserve and perpetuate memorials of the history of the state by parks, buildings, monuments, statues, paintings, documents of historical value or by other means, and to preserve places of historic or archaeological interest or scenic beauty, and for such purposes private property or the use thereof may be acquired by gift, purchase, or eminent domain or be subjected to reasonable regulation or control.

INITIATIVE AND REFERENDUM

Section 49. Reservation of Power to Enact and Reject Laws

The people reserve power to propose and enact or reject laws and amendments to the constitution by the initiative, independent of the general assembly, and also reserve power to approve or reject by referendum any act of the general assembly, except as hereinafter provided. Source: Const. of 1875, Art. IV, Sec. 57 (Amended November 3, 1908). Section 50. Initiative petitions—signatures required—form and procedure.— Initiative petitions proposing amendments to the constitution shall be signed by eight percent of the legal voters in each of two-thirds of the congressional districts in the state, and petitions proposing laws shall be signed by five percent of such voters. Every such petition shall be filed with the secretary of state not less than six months before the election and shall contain an enacting clause and the full text of the measure. Petitions for constitutional amendments shall not contain more than one amended and revised article of this constitution, or one new article which shall not contain more than one subject and matters properly connected therewith, and the enacting clause thereof shall be "be it resolved by the people of the state of Missouri that the Constitution be amended:". Petitions for laws shall contain not more than one subject which shall be expressed clearly in the title, and the enacting clause thereof shall be "be it enacted by the people of the state of Missouri:".

Section 51. Appropriations by Initiative—Effective Date of Initiated Laws— Conflicting Laws Concurrently Adopted

The initiative shall not be used for the appropriation of money other than of new revenues created and provided for thereby, or for any other purpose prohibited by this constitution. Except as provided in this constitution, any measure proposed shall take effect when approved by a majority of the votes cast thereon. When conflicting measures are approved at the same election the one receiving the largest affirmative vote shall prevail.

Section 52(A). Referendum—Exceptions—Procedure

A referendum may be ordered (except as to laws necessary for the immediate preservation of the public peace, health or safety, and laws making appropriations for the current expenses of the state government, for the maintenance of state institutions and for the support of public schools) either by petitions signed by five percent of the legal voters in each of two-thirds of the congressional districts in the state, or by the general assembly, as other bills are enacted. Referendum petitions shall be filed with the secretary of state not more than ninety days after the final adjournment of the session of the general assembly which passed the bill on which the referendum is demanded.

Section 52(B). Veto Power—Elections—Effective Date

The veto power of the governor shall not extend to measures referred to the people. All elections on measures referred to the people shall be had at the general state elections, except when the general assembly shall order a special election. Any measure referred to the people shall take effect when approved by a majority of the votes cast thereon, and not otherwise. This section shall not be construed to deprive any member of the general assembly of the right to introduce any measure.

Section 53. Basis for Computation of Signatures Required

The total vote for governor at the general election last preceding the filing of any initiative or referendum petition shall be used to determine the number of legal voters necessary to sign the petition. in submitting the same to the people the secretary of state and all other officers shall be governed by general laws.

ARTICLE IV: EXECUTIVE DEPARTMENT

Section 1. Executive Power—The Governor

The supreme executive power shall be vested in a governor.

Section 2. Duties of Governor

The governor shall take care that the laws are distributed and faithfully executed, and shall be a conservator of the peace throughout the state.

Section 3. Qualifications of Governor

The governor shall be at least thirty years old and shall have been a citizen of the United States for at least fifteen years and a resident of this state at least ten years next before election.

Section 4. Power of Appointment to Fill Vacancies—Tenure of Appointees

The governor shall fill all vacancies in public offices unless otherwise provided by law, and his appointees shall serve until their successors are duly elected or appointed and qualified.

Section 5. Commissions of State Officers

The governor shall commission all officers unless otherwise provided by law. All commissions shall be issued in the name of the state, signed by the governor, sealed with the great seal of the state and attested by the secretary of state.

Section 6. Commander in Chief of Militia—Authority

The governor shall be the commander in chief of the militia, except when it is called into the service of the United States, and may call out the militia to execute the laws, suppress actual and prevent threatened insurrection, and repel invasion.

Section 7. Reprieves, Commutations and Pardons—Limitations On Power

The governor shall have power to grant reprieves, commutations and pardons, after conviction, for all offenses except treason and cases of impeachment, upon such conditions and with such restrictions and limitations as he may deem proper, subject to provisions of law as to the manner of applying for pardons. The power to pardon shall not include the power to parole.

Section 8. Concurrent Resolutions—Duty of Governor—Exceptions—Limitation of Effect

Every resolution to which the concurrence of the senate and house of representatives may be necessary, except on questions of adjournment, going into joint session, and of amending this constitution, shall be presented to the governor, and before the same shall take effect, shall be proceeded upon in the same manner as in the case of a bill; provided, that no resolution shall have the effect to repeal, extend, or amend any law.

Section 9. Governor's Messages and Recommendations to Assembly—Call of Extra Sessions

The governor shall, at the commencement of each session of the general assembly, at the close of his term of office, and at such other times as he may deem necessary, give to the general assembly information as to the state of the government, and shall recommend to its consideration such measures as he shall deem necessary and expedient. On extraordinary occasions he may convene the general assembly by proclamation, wherein he shall state specifically each matter on which action is deemed necessary.

Section 10. Lieutenant Governor—Qualifications, Powers and Duties

There shall be a lieutenant governor who shall have the same qualifications as the governor and shall be ex officio president of the senate. in committee of the whole he may debate all questions, and shall cast the deciding vote on equal division in the senate and on joint vote of both houses.

Section 11(A). Order of Succession to Governorship, When

If the governor-elect dies before taking office, the lieutenant governor-elect shall take the term of the governor-elect. On the death, conviction or impeachment, or resignation of the governor, the lieutenant governor shall become governor for the remainder of the term. If there be no lieutenant governor the president pro tempore of the senate, the speaker of the house, the secretary of state, the state auditor, the state treasurer or the attorney general in succession shall become governor. On the failure to qualify, absence from the state or other disability of the governor, the powers, duties and emoluments of the governor shall devolve upon the lieutenant governor for the remainder of the term or until the disability is removed. If there be no lieutenant governor, or for any of said causes the lieutenant governor is incapable of acting, the president pro tempore of the senate, the speaker of the house, the secretary of state, the state auditor, the state treasurer, and the attorney general in succession shall act as governor until the disability is removed.

Section 11(B). Governor's Declaration of Disability, Effect of—Disability Board, Membership, Duties—Governor to Resume Office, When—Disputed Illness, Supreme Court to Decide

Whenever the governor transmits to the president pro tempore of the senate and the speaker of the house of representatives his written declaration that he is unable to discharge the powers and duties of his office, and until he transmits to them a written declaration to the contrary, such powers and duties shall be discharged by the lieutenant governor, or if there be no lieutenant governor, by the president pro tempore of the senate, the speaker of the house, secretary of state, the state auditor, the state treasurer, or the attorney general in succession, as acting governor. Whenever a majority of a disability board comprised of the lieutenant governor, the secretary of state, the state auditor, the state treasurer, the attorney general, president pro tempore of the senate, the speaker of the house of representatives, the majority floor leader of the senate, and majority floor leader of the house, transmits to the president pro tempore of the senate and the speaker of the house of representatives their written declaration that the governor is unable to discharge the powers and duties of his office, the lieutenant governor, or if there be no lieutenant governor, the president pro tempore of the senate, the speaker of the house, the secretary of state, the state auditor, the state treasurer or the attorney general in succession, shall immediately assume the powers and duties of the office as acting governor. Thereafter when the governor transmits to the disability board his written declaration that no inability exists, he shall resume the powers and duties of his office on the fourth day after he transmits such declaration unless a majority of the disability board transmits their written declaration that the governor is unable to discharge the powers and duties of his office to the supreme court within that four day period, and the supreme court shall then convene to decide the issue. If the supreme court within twenty-one days after receipt of such declaration, determines by a majority vote of all members thereof that the governor is unable to discharge the powers and duties of his office, the acting governor shall continue to discharge the same as acting governor; otherwise, the governor shall resume the powers and duties of his office.

Section 11(C). Acting As Governor Not to Vacate Regular Office

If any state officer other than the lieutenant governor is acting as governor, his regular elective office shall not be deemed vacant and all duties of that office shall be performed by his chief administrative assistant.

Section 12. Executive Department, Composition of—Elective Officials—Departments and Offices Enumerated

The executive department shall consist of all state elective and appointive officials and employees except officials and employees of the legislative and judicial departments. in addition to the governor and lieutenant governor there shall be a state auditor, secretary of state, attorney general, a state treasurer, an office of administration, a department of agriculture, a department of conservation, a department of natural resources, a department of elementary and secondary education, a department of higher education, a department of highways and transportation, a department of insurance, a department of labor and industrial relations, a department of economic development, a department of public safety, a department of revenue, a department of social services, and a department of mental health. in addition to the elected officers, there shall not be more than fifteen departments and the office of administration. The general assembly may create by law two departments, in addition to those named, provided that the departments shall be headed by a director or commission appointed by the governor on the advice and consent of the senate. The director or commission shall have administrative responsibility and authority for the department created by law. Unless discontinued all present or future boards, bureaus, commissions and other agencies of the state exercising administrative or executive authority shall be assigned by law or by the governor as provided by law to the office of administration or to one of the fifteen administrative departments to which their respective powers and duties are germane.

Section 13. State Auditor—Qualifications and Duties—Limitations On Du Ties

The state auditor shall have the same qualifications as the governor. He shall establish appropriate systems of accounting for all public officials of the state, post-audit the accounts of all state agencies and audit the treasury at least once annually. He shall make all other audits and investigations required by law, and shall make an annual report to the governor and general assembly. He shall establish appropriate systems of accounting for the political subdivisions of the state, supervise their budgeting systems, and audit their accounts as provided by law. No duty shall be imposed on him by law which is not related to the supervising and auditing of the receipt and expenditure of public funds.

Section 14. Secretary of State—Duties—State Seal—Official Register—Limitation On Duties

The secretary of state shall be custodian of the seal of the state, and authenticate therewith all official acts of the governor except the approval of laws. The seal shall be called the "Great Seal of the State of Missouri," and its present emblems and devices shall not be subject to change. He shall keep a register of the official acts of the governor, attest them when necessary, and when required shall lay copies thereof, and of all papers relative thereto, before either house of the general assembly. He shall be custodian of such records, and documents and perform such duties in relation thereto, and in relation to elections and corporations, as provided by law, but no duty shall be imposed on him by law which is not related to his duties as prescribed in this constitution.

Section 15. State Treasurer—Duties—Custody, Investment and Deposit of State Funds—Duties Limited—Non-state Funds to be in Custody and Invested by Department of Revenue—Non-state Funds Defined

The state treasurer shall be custodian of all state funds and funds received from the United States government. The department of revenue shall take custody of and invest nonstate funds as defined herein, and other moneys authorized to be held by the department of revenue. All revenue collected and moneys received by the state which are state funds or funds received from the United States government shall go promptly into the state treasury. All revenue collected and moneys received by the department of revenue which are nonstate funds as defined herein shall be promptly credited to the fund provided by law for that type of money. Immediately upon receipt of state or United States funds the state treasurer shall deposit all moneys in the state treasury in banking institutions selected by him and approved by the governor and state auditor, and he shall hold them for the benefit of the respective funds to which they belong and disburse them as provided by law. Unless otherwise provided by law, all interest received on nonstate funds shall be credited to such funds. The state treasurer shall determine by the exercise of his best judgment the amount of moneys in his custody that are not needed for current expenses and shall place all such moneys on time deposit, bearing interest, in banking institutions in this state selected by the state treasurer and approved by the governor and state auditor or in obligations of the United States government or any agency or instrumentality thereof maturing and becoming payable not more than five years from the date of purchase. in addition the treasurer may enter into repurchase agreements maturing and becoming payable within ninety days secured by United States Treasury obligations or obligations of United States government agencies or instrumentalities of any maturity, as provided by law. The treasurer may also invest in banker's acceptances issued by domestic commercial banks possessing the highest rating issued by a nationally recognized rating agency and in commercial paper issued by domestic corporations which has received the highest rating issued by a nationally recognized rating agency. Investments in banker's acceptances and commercial paper shall mature and become payable not more than one hundred eighty days from the date of purchase, maintain the highest rating throughout the duration of the investment and meet any other requirements provided by law. The state treasurer shall prepare, maintain and adhere to a written investment policy which shall include an asset allocation plan limiting the total amount of state money which may be invested in each investment category authorized by this section. The investment and deposit of state, United States and nonstate funds shall be subject to such restrictions and requirements as may be prescribed by law. Banking institutions in which state and United States funds are deposited by the state treasurer shall give security satisfactory to the governor, state auditor and state treasurer for the safekeeping and payment of the deposits and interest thereon pursuant to deposit agreements made with the state treasurer pursuant to law. No duty shall be imposed on the state treasurer by law which is not related to the receipt, investment, custody and disbursement of state funds and funds received from the United States government. As used in the section, the term "banking institutions" shall include banks, trust companies, savings and loan associations, credit unions, production credit associations authorized by act of the United States Congress, and other financial institutions which are authorized by law to accept funds for deposit or which in the case of production credit associations, issues securities. As used in this section, the term "nonstate funds" shall include all taxes and fees imposed by political subdivisions and collected by the department of revenue; all taxes which are imposed by the state, collected by the department of revenue and distributed by the department of revenue to political subdivisions; and all other moneys which are hereafter designated as "nonstate funds" to be administered by the department of revenue.

Section 16. Filing of Administrative Rules and Regulations

All rules and regulations of any board or other administrative agency of the executive department, except those relating to its organization and internal management, shall take effect not less than ten days after the filing thereof in the office of the secretary of state.

Section 17. Elective State Officers—Time of Election and Terms—Limitation On Reelection—Selection of Department Heads—Removal and Qualifications of Appointive Officers

The governor, lieutenant governor, secretary of state, state treasurer and attorney general shall be elected at the presidential elections for terms of four years each. The state auditor shall be elected for a term of two years at the general election in the year 1948, and his successors shall be elected for terms of four years. No person shall be elected governor or treasurer more than twice, and no person who has held the office of governor or treasurer, or acted as governor or treasurer, for more than two years of a term to which some other person was elected to the office of governor or treasurer shall be elected to the office of governor or treasurer more than once. The heads of all the executive departments shall be appointed by the governor, by and with the advice and consent of the senate. All appointive officers may be removed by the governor and shall possess the qualifications required by this constitution or by law.

Section 18. Election Returns—Board of State Canvassers—Time of Meeting and Duties—Requirement for Election—Tie Votes

The returns of every election for governor, lieutenant governor, secretary of state, state auditor, state treasurer and attorney general shall be sealed and transmitted by the returning officers to the secretary of state, who shall appoint two disinterested judges of a court of record of the state, and the three shall constitute a board of state canvassers. The board shall meet at the state capitol on, or at the call of the secretary of state before, the second Tuesday of December next after the election and forthwith open and canvass the returns of the votes cast and from the face thereof ascertain and proclaim the result of the election. The persons having the highest number of votes for the respective offices shall be declared elected, and if two or more persons have an equal and the highest number of votes for the same office, at its next regular session the general assembly, by joint vote and without delay, shall choose one of such persons for the office.

Section 19. Department Personnel—Selection and Removal—Merit System— Veterans' Preference

The head of each department may select and remove all appointees in the department except as otherwise provided in this constitution, or by law. All employees in the state eleemosynary and penal institutions, and other state employees as provided by law, shall be selected on the basis of merit, ascertained as nearly as practicable by competitive examinations; provided that any honorably discharged member of the armed services of the United States who is a citizen of this state shall have preference in examination and appointment as prescribed by law.

Section 20. Location of Executive and Administrative Offices

The executive and administrative officials and departments herein provided for shall establish their principal offices and keep all necessary public records, books and papers at the City of Jefferson.

Section 21. Limitation On Changes of Salaries—Fees, Costs

The officers named in this article shall receive for their services salaries fixed by law, which shall not be increased or diminished during their terms. After the expiration of the terms of those now in office the officers named shall not receive to their own use any fees, costs, perquisites of office or other compensation, and all fees provided by law for any service performed by them shall be paid in advance into the state treasury.

REVENUE

Section 22. Department of Revenue, Duties of—Director, Appointment of

The department of revenue shall be in charge of a director of revenue appointed by the governor, by and with the advice and consent of the senate. The department shall have divisions as provided by law. The department shall collect all taxes and fees payable to the state as provided by law.

Section 23. Fiscal Year—Limitations On Appropriations—Specification of Amount and Purpose

The fiscal year of the state and all its agencies shall be the twelve months beginning on the first day of July in each year. The general assembly shall make appropriations for one or two fiscal years, and the sixty-third general assembly shall also make appropriations for the six months ending June 30, 1945. Every appropriation law shall distinctly specify the amount and purpose of the appropriation without reference to any other law to fix the amount or purpose.

Section 24. Governor's Budget and Recommendations As to Revenue—Proposed Legislation Not Enacted Not to be Included in Projection of New Revenues

The governor shall, within thirty days after it convenes in each regular session, submit to the general assembly a budget for the ensuing appropriation period, containing the estimated available revenues of the state and a complete and itemized plan of proposed expenditures of the state and all its agencies. The governor shall not determine estimated available revenues of the state using any projection of new revenues to be created from proposed legislation that has not been passed into law by the general assembly. Estimates of any unspent fund balances, without regard to actual or estimated revenues but accounting for all existing appropriations, that will constitute a surplus during the fiscal year immediately preceding the fiscal year or years for which the governor is recommending a budget, may be included in the estimated revenue available for expenditure during the fiscal year or years for which the governor is recommending a budget. As used in this section, new revenues shall not include existing provisions of law subject to expiration during the ensuing appropriation period.

Section 25. Limitation of Governor's Budget On Power of Appropriations

Until it acts on all the appropriations recommended in the budget, neither house of the general assembly shall pass any appropriation other than emergency appropriations recommended by the governor.

Section 26. Power of Partial Veto of Appropriation Bills—Procedure—Limitations

The governor may object to one or more items or portions of items of appropriation of money in any bill presented to him, while approving other portions of the bill. On signing it he shall append to the bill a statement of the items or portions of items to which he objects and such items or portions shall not take effect. If the general assembly be in session he shall transmit to the house in which the bill originated a copy of the statement, and the items or portions objected to shall be reconsidered separately. If it be not in session he shall transmit the bill within forty-five days to the office of the secretary of state with his approval or reasons for disapproval. The governor shall not reduce any appropriation for free public schools, or for the payment of principal and interest on the public debt.

Section 27. Power of Governor to Control Rate of and Reduce Expenditures — Notification to General Assembly, When

1. The governor may control the rate at which any appropriation is expended during the period of the appropriation by allotment and may reduce the expenditures of the state or any of its agencies below their appropriations whenever the actual revenues are less than the revenue estimates upon which the appropriations were based. The governor shall not reduce any appropriation for the payment of principal and interest on the public debt.

2. The governor shall notify the general assembly by proclamation whenever the rate at which any appropriation shall be expended is not equal quarterly allotments, the sum of which shall be equal to the amount of the appropriation. Any rate of expenditure for any appropriation which is not equal quarterly allotments shall stand reconsidered in the chamber in which the bill that contained the appropriation originated. Such reconsideration shall be in the manner that a bill is reconsidered under article III, section 32. Either the general assembly that receives the proclamation or the next general assembly may reconsider the rate of expenditure. If the general assembly successfully reconsiders the rate of expenditure for the appropriation in question, the rate shall be assumed to be equal quarterly allotments. Such reconsideration may be at any time the general assembly is in session including sessions pursuant to article III, sections 20, 20(b), and 32 and article IV, section 9. Either the general assembly that receives the proclamation or the next general assembly may reconsider such allotment allocation change. Such reconsideration may be at any time the general assembly is in session including sessions pursuant to article III, sections 20, 20(b), and 32 and article IV, section 9.

3. The governor shall notify the general assembly by proclamation when the governor reduces one or more items or portions of items of appropriation of money as a result of actual revenues being less than the revenue estimates upon which the appropriations were based. Each item or portions of items of appropriation of money shall stand reconsidered in the chamber in which the bill that contained the appropriation originated. Such reconsideration shall be in the manner that a bill is reconsidered under article III, section 32. Either the general assembly that receives the proclamation or the next general assembly may reconsider such reduction. Such reconsideration may be at any time the general assembly is in session including sessions pursuant to article III, sections 20, 20(b), and 32 and article IV, section 9.

Section 27(A). Budget Reserve Fund Established—Investment—Excess Transfer to General Revenue, When

1. There is hereby established within the state treasury a fund to be known as the "Budget Reserve Fund". The balances in the cash operating reserve fund and the budget stabilization fund shall be transferred to the budget reserve fund.

2. The commissioner of administration may, throughout any fiscal year, transfer amounts from the budget reserve fund to the general revenue fund or any other state fund without other legislative action if he determines that such amounts are necessary for the cash requirements of this state. Such transfers shall be deemed "cash operating transfers".

3. The commissioner of administration shall transfer from the general revenue fund or other recipient fund to the budget reserve fund an amount equal to the cash operating transfer received by such fund pursuant to subsection 2 of this section, together with the interest that would have been earned on such amount, prior to May sixteenth of the fiscal year in which the transfer was made. No cash operating transfers out of the budget reserve fund may be made after May fifteenth of any fiscal year.

4. Funds in the budget reserve fund shall be invested by the treasurer in the same manner as other state funds are invested. Interest earned on such investments shall be credited to the budget reserve fund. Subject to the provisions of subsection 7 of this section, the unexpended balance in the budget reserve fund at the close of any fiscal year shall remain in the fund.

5. in any fiscal year in which the governor reduces the expenditures of the state or any of its agencies below their appropriations in accordance with section 27 of this article, or in which there is a budget need due to a disaster, as proclaimed by the governor to be an emergency, the general assembly, upon a request by the governor for an emergency appropriation and by a two-thirds vote of the members elected to each house, may appropriate funds from the budget reserve fund to fulfill the expenditures authorized by any of the existing appropriations which were affected by the governor's decision to reduce expenditures pursuant to section 27 of this article or to meet budget needs due to the disaster. Such expenditures shall be deemed to be for "budget stabilization purposes". The maximum amount which may be appropriated at any one time for such budget stabilization purposes shall be one-half of the sum of the balance in the fund and any amounts appropriated or otherwise owed to the fund, less all amounts owed to the fund for budget stabilization purposes but not yet appropriated for repayment to the fund.

6. One-third of the amount transferred or expended from the budget reserve fund for budget stabilization purposes during any fiscal year, together with interest that would otherwise have been earned on such amount, shall stand appropriated to the budget reserve fund during each of the next three fiscal years, and such amount, and any additional amounts which may be appropriated for that purpose, shall be transferred from the fund which received such transfer to the budget reserve fund by the fifteenth day of the fiscal year for each of the next three fiscal years or until the full amount, plus interest, has been returned to the budget reserve fund. The maximum amount, which may be outstanding at any one time and subject to repayment to the budget reserve fund for budget stabilization purposes shall be one-half of the sum of the balance in the fund and all outstanding amounts appropriated or otherwise owed to the fund.

7. If the balance in the budget reserve fund at the close of any fiscal year exceeds seven and one-half percent of the net general revenue collections for the previous fiscal year, the commissioner of administration shall transfer that excess amount to the general revenue fund unless such excess balance is as a result of direct appropriations made by the general assembly for the purpose of increasing the balance of the fund; provided, however, that if the balance in the fund at the close of any fiscal year exceeds ten percent of the net general revenue collections for the previous fiscal year, the commissioner of administration shall transfer the excess amount to the general revenue fund notwithstanding any specific appropriations made to the fund. for purposes of this section, "net general revenue collections" means all revenue deposited into the general revenue fund less refunds and revenues originally deposited into the general revenue fund but designated by law for a specific distribution or transfer to another state fund. 8. If the sum of the ending balance of the budget reserve fund in any fiscal year and any amounts owed to the fund pursuant to subsection 6 of this section is less than seven and one-half percent of the net general revenue collections for the same year, the difference shall stand appropriated and shall be transferred from the general revenue fund to the budget reserve fund by the fifteenth day of the succeeding fiscal year.

Section 27(B). Facilities Maintenance and Review Fund Created, Purpose—State Facilities, Defined—Transfer of Monies Into Fund, Reduction Or Elimination of Transfer by Governor

1. The "Facilities Maintenance Reserve Fund" is hereby created in the state treasury for use in maintaining, repairing and renovating state facilities. "State facilities" shall include all improvements to real property owned by the state except real property owned or possessed by the conservation and highways and transportation commissions, including bridges and highways constructed pursuant to article IV, section 29.

2. Beginning July 1, 1997, moneys shall be transferred from the general revenue fund to the facilities maintenance reserve fund. The amount transferred in fiscal year 1998 shall be equal to one-tenth of one percent of net general revenue collections of fiscal year 1997. During each succeeding fiscal year the percentage of the immediately preceding fiscal year's net general revenue collections to be transferred to the facilities maintenance reserve fund shall be increased by one-tenth of one percent, until the total percentage transferred equals one percent of the net general revenue collections for the immediately preceding fiscal year. Each year thereafter one percent of the net general revenue collections for the immediately preceding fiscal year shall be transferred to the facilities maintenance reserve fund; provided, however, that the governor may reduce or eliminate the amount of this transfer during any fiscal year in which he exercised his right to reduce expenditures pursuant to article IV, section 27, or during the next succeeding fiscal year after he exercised such power. The general assembly may also appropriate other moneys to the fund.

3. Moneys in the facilities maintenance reserve fund shall be invested by the state treasurer in the same manner as other state funds are invested. Interest earned on such investments shall be credited to the facilities reserve maintenance fund.

4. The general assembly may appropriate moneys from the fund to be used for maintenance, repair or renovation of state facilities.

Section 28. Treasury Withdrawals, How Made, Certified How—Appropriation, Period of

No money shall be withdrawn from the state treasury except by warrant drawn in accordance with an appropriation made by law, nor shall any obligation for that payment of money be incurred unless the commissioner of administration certifies it for payment and certifies that the expenditure is within the purpose as directed by the general assembly of the appropriation and that there is in the appropriation an unencumbered balance sufficient to pay it. At the time of issuance each such certification shall be entered on the general accounting books as an encumbrance on the appropriation. No appropriation shall confer authority to incur an obligation after the termination of the fiscal period to which it relates, and every appropriation shall expire six months after the end of the period for which made.

HIGHWAYS AND TRANSPORTATION

Section 29. Highways and Transportation Commission—Qualifications of Members and Employees—Authority Over State Highways and Other Transportation Programs

The highways and transportation commission shall be in charge of the department of transportation. The number, qualifications, compensation and terms of the members of the highways and transportation commission shall be fixed by law, and not more than one-half of its members shall be of the same political party. The selection and removal of all employees shall be without regard to political affiliation. The highways and transportation commission:

(i) shall have authority over the state highway system;

(ii) shall have authority over all other transportation programs and facilities as provided by law, including, but not limited to, aviation, railroads, mass transportation, ports, and waterborne commerce; and

(iii) shall have authority to limit access to, from and across state highways and other transportation facilities where the public interests and safety may require. All references to the highway commission and the department of highways in this constitution and in the statutes shall mean the highways and transportation commission and the department of transportation.

Section 30(A). Apportionment of Motor Vehicle Fuel Tax—Director of Revenue Responsible for Apportionment—Limitation On Local Fuel Taxes—Fuel Taxes Not Part of Total State Revenues Or Expenses of State Government

1. A tax upon or measured by fuel used for propelling highway motor vehicles shall be levied and collected as provided by law. Any amount of the tax collected with respect to fuel not used for propelling highway motor vehicles shall be refunded by the state in the manner provided by law. The remaining net proceeds of the tax, after deducting actual costs of collection of the department of revenue (but after June 30, 2005, not more than three percent of the amount collected) and refunds for overpayments and erroneous payments of such tax as permitted by law, shall be apportioned and distributed between the counties, cities and the state highways and transportation commission as hereinafter provided and shall stand appropriated without legislative action for the following purposes:

(1) Ten percent of the remaining net proceeds shall be deposited in a special trust fund known as the "County Aid Road Trust Fund". in addition, beginning July 1, 1994, an additional five percent of the remaining net proceeds which is derived from the difference between the amount received from a tax rate equal to the tax rate in effect on March 31, 1992, and the tax rate in effect on and after July 1, 1994, shall also be deposited in the county aid road trust fund, and of such moneys generated by this additional five percent, five percent shall be apportioned and distributed solely to cities not within any county in this state. After such distribution to cities not within any county, the remaining proceeds in the county aid road trust fund shall be apportioned and distributed to the various counties of the state on the following basis: One-half on the ratio that the county road mileage of each county bears to the county road mileage of the entire state as determined by the last available report of the state highways and transportation commission and one-half on the ratio that the rural land valuation of each county bears to the rural land valuation of the entire state as determined by the last available report of the state tax commission, except that county road mileage in incorporated villages, towns or cities and the land valuation in incorporated villages, towns or cities shall be excluded in such determination, except that, if the assessed valuation of rural lands in any county is less than five million dollars, the county shall be treated as having an assessed valuation of five million dollars. The funds apportioned and distributed to each county shall be dedicated, used and expended by the county solely for the construction, reconstruction, maintenance and repairs of roads, bridges and highways, and subject to such other provisions and restrictions as provided by law. The moneys generated by the additional five percent of the remaining net proceeds which is derived from the difference between the amount received from a tax rate equal to the tax rate in effect on March 31, 1992, and the tax rate in effect on and after July 1, 1994, shall not be used or expended for equipment, machinery, salaries, fringe benefits or capital improvements, other than roads and bridges. in counties having the township form of county organization, the funds distributed to such counties shall be expended solely under the control and supervision of the county commission, and shall not be expended by the various townships located within such counties. "Rural land" as used in this section shall mean all land located within any county, except land in incorporated villages, towns, or cities.

(2) Fifteen percent of the remaining net proceeds shall be apportioned and distributed to the various incorporated cities, towns and villages within the state solely for construction, reconstruction, maintenance, repair, policing, signing, lighting and cleaning roads and streets and for the payment of principal and interest on indebtedness on account of road and street purposes, and the use thereof being subject to such other provisions and restrictions as provided by law. The amount apportioned and uted to each city, town or village shall be based on the ratio that the population of the city, town or village bears to the population of all incorporated cities, towns or villages in the state having a like population, as shown by the last federal decennial census, provided that any city, town or village which had a motor fuel tax prior to the adoption of this section shall annually receive not less than an amount equal to the net revenue derived therefrom in the year 1960; and

(3) All the remaining net proceeds in excess of the distributions to counties, and to cities, towns and villages under this section shall be apportioned, distributed and deposited in the state road fund and shall be expended and used solely as provided in subsection 1 of section 30(b) of Article IV of this Constitution. 2. The director of revenue of the state shall make the apportionment, distribution and deposit of the funds monthly in the manner required hereby.

3. Except for taxes or licenses which may be imposed uniformly on all merchants or manufacturers based upon sales, or which uniformly apply ad valorem to the stocks of merchants or manufacturers, no political subdivision in this state shall collect any tax, excise, license or fee upon, measured by or with respect to the importation, receipt, manufacture, storage, transportation, sale or use, on or after the first day of the month next following the adoption of this section of fuel used for propelling motor vehicles, unless the tax, excise, license or fee is approved by a vote of the people of any city, town or village subsequent to the adoption of this section, by a two- thirds majority. All funds collected shall be used solely for construction, reconstruction, maintenance, repair, policing, signing, lighting, and cleaning roads and streets and for the payment and interest on indebtedness incurred on account of road and street purposes. 4. The net proceeds of fuel taxes apportioned, distributed and deposited under this section to the state road fund, counties, cities, towns and villages shall not be included within the definition of "total state revenues" in section 17 of article X of this constitution nor be considered as an "expense of state government" as that term is used in section 20 of article X of this constitution.

Section 30(B). Source and Application of State Road Fund—Sales Tax Imposed On Sale of Motor Vehicles, Apportionment, How, Use of Revenue—Distribution of Increases—Sales Taxes Not Part of Total State Revenues Or Expenses of State Government

1. for the purpose of constructing and maintaining an adequate system of connected state highways all state revenue derived from highway users as an incident to their use or right to use the highways of the state, including all state license fees and taxes upon motor vehicles, trailers and motor vehicle fuels, and upon, with respect to, or on the privilege of the manufacture, receipt, storage, distribution, sale or use thereof (excepting those portions of the sales tax on motor vehicles and trailers which are not distributed to the state road fund pursuant to subsection 2 of this section 30(b) and further excepting all property taxes), less the

(1) actual cost of collection of the department of revenue (but not to exceed three percent of the particular tax or fee collected),

(2) actual cost of refunds for overpayments and erroneous payments of such taxes and fees and maintaining retirement programs as permitted by law and

(3) actual cost of the state highway patrol in administering and enforcing any state motor vehicle laws and traffic regulations, shall be deposited in the state road fund which is hereby created within the state treasury and stand appropriated without legislative action to be used and expended by the highways and transportation commission for the following purposes, and no other: First, to the payment of the principal and interest on any outstanding state road bonds. The term state road bonds in this section 30(b) means any bonds or refunding bonds issued by the highways and transportation commission to finance or refinance the construction or reconstruction of the state highway system. Second, to maintain a balance in the state road fund in the amount deemed necessary to meet the payment of the principal and interest of any state road bonds for the next succeeding twelve months. The remaining balance in the state road fund shall be used and expended in the sole discretion of and under the supervision and direction of the highways and transportation commission for the following state highway system uses and purposes and no other:

(1) to complete and widen or otherwise improve and maintain the state highway system heretofore designated and laid out under existing laws;

(2) to reimburse the various counties and other political subdivisions of the state, except incorporated cities and towns, for money expended by them in the construction or acquisition of roads and bridges now or hereafter taken over by the highways and transportation commission as permanent parts of the state highway system, to the extent of the value to the state of such roads and bridges at the time taken over, not exceeding in any case the amount expended by such counties and subdivisions in the construction or acquisition of such roads and bridges, except that the highways and transportation commission may, in its discretion, repay, or agree to repay, any cash advanced by a county or subdivision to expedite state road construction or improvement;

(3) in the discretion of the commission to plan, locate, relocate, establish, acquire, construct and maintain the following:

(a) interstate and primary highways within the state;

(b) supplementary state highways and bridges in each county of the state;

(c) state highways and bridges in, to and through state parks, public areas and reservations, and state institutions now or hereafter established to connect the same with the state highways, and also national, state or local parkways, travelways, tourways, with coordinated facilities;

(d) any tunnel or interstate bridge or part thereof, where necessary to connect the state highways of this state with those of other states;

(e) any highway within the state when necessary to comply with any federal law or requirement which is or shall become a condition to the receipt of federal funds;

(f) any highway in any city or town which is found necessary as a continuation of any state or federal highway, or any connection therewith, into and through such city or town; and

(g) additional state highways, bridges and tunnels, either in congested traffic areas of the state or where needed to facilitate and expedite the movement of through traffic.

(4) to acquire materials, equipment and buildings and to employ such personnel as necessary for the purposes described in this subsection 1; and

(5) for such other purposes and contingencies relating and appertaining to the construction and maintenance of such state highway system as the highways and transportation commission may deem necessary and proper.

2. (1) The state sales tax upon the sale of motor vehicles, trailers, motorcycles, mopeds and motortricycles at the rate provided by law on November 2, 2004, is levied and imposed by this section until the rate is changed by law or constitutional amendment.

(2) One-half of the proceeds from the state sales tax on all motor vehicles, trailers, motorcycles, mopeds and motortricycles shall be dedicated for highway and transportation use and shall be apportioned and distributed as follows: ten percent to the counties, fifteen percent to the cities, two percent to be deposited in the state transportation fund, which is hereby created within the state treasury to be used in a manner provided by law and seventy-three percent to be deposited in the state road fund. The amounts apportioned and distributed to the counties and cities shall be further allocated and used as provided in section 30(a) of this article. The amounts allocated and distributed to the highways and transportation commission for the state road fund shall be used as provided in subsection 1 of this section 30(b). The sales taxes which are apportioned and distributed pursuant to this subdivision (2) shall not include those taxes levied and imposed pursuant to sections 43(a) or 47(a) of this article. The term "proceeds from the state sales tax" as used in this subdivision (2) shall mean and include all revenues received by the department of revenue from the said sales tax, reduced only by refunds for overpayments and erroneous payments of such tax as permitted by law and actual costs of collection by the department of revenue (but not to exceed three percent of the amount collected).

(3) (i) From and after July 1, 2005, through June 30, 2006, twenty-five percent of the remaining one-half of the proceeds of the state sales tax on all motor vehicles, trailers, motorcycles, mopeds and motortricycles which is not distributed by subdivision (2) of subsection 2 of this section 30(b) shall be deposited in the state road bond fund which is hereby created within the state treasury;

(ii) from and after July 1, 2006, through June 30, 2007, fifty percent of the aforesaid one-half of the proceeds of the state sales tax on all motor vehicles, trailers, motorcycles, mopeds and motortricycles which is not distributed by subdivision (2) of subsection 2 of this section 30(b) shall be deposited in the state road bond fund; (iii) from and after July 1, 2007, through June 30, 2008, seventy-five percent of the aforesaid one- half of the proceeds of the state sales tax on all motor vehicles, trailers, motorcycles, mopeds and motortricycles which is not distributed by subdivision (2) of subsection 2 of this section 30(b) shall be deposited in the state road bond fund; and (iv) from and after July 1, 2008, one hundred percent of the aforesaid one-half of the proceeds of the state sales tax on all motor vehicles, trailers, motorcycles, mopeds and motortricycles which is not distributed by subdivision (2) of subsection 2 of this section 30(b) shall be deposited in the state road bond fund. Moneys deposited in the state road bond fund are hereby dedicated to and shall only be used to fund the repayment of bonds issued by the highways and transportation commission to fund the construction and reconstruction of the state highway system or to fund refunding bonds, except that after January 1, 2009, that portion of the moneys in the state road bond fund which the commissioner of administration and the highways and transportation commission each certify is not needed to make payments upon said bonds or to maintain an adequate reserve for making future payments upon said bonds may be appropriated to the state road fund. The highways and transportation commission shall have authority to issue state road bonds for the uses set forth in this subdivision (3). The net proceeds received from the issuance of such bonds shall be paid into the state road fund and shall only be used to fund construction or reconstruction of specific projects for parts of the state highway system as determined by the highways and transportation commission. The moneys deposited in the state road bond fund shall only be withdrawn by appropriation pursuant to this constitution. No obligation for the payment of moneys so appropriated shall be paid unless the commissioner of administration certifies it for payment and further certifies that the expenditure is for a use which is specifically authorized by the provisions of this subdivision (3). The proceeds of the sales tax which are subject to allocation and deposit into the state road bond fund pursuant to this subdivision (3) shall not include the proceeds of the sales tax levied and imposed pursuant to sections 43(a) or 47(a) of this article nor shall they include the proceeds of that portion of the sales tax apportioned, distributed and dedicated to the school district trust fund on November 2, 2004. The term "proceeds from the state sales tax" as used in this subdivision (3) shall mean and include all revenues received by the department of revenue from the said sales tax, reduced only by refunds for overpayments and erroneous payments of such tax as permitted by law and actual costs of collection by the department of revenue (but not to exceed three percent of the amount collected).

3. After January 1, 1980, any increase in state license fees and taxes on motor vehicles, trailers, motorcycles, mopeds and motortricycles other than those taxes distributed pursuant to subsection 2 of this section 30(b) shall be distributed as follows: ten percent to the counties, fifteen percent to the cities and seventy-five percent to be deposited in the state road fund. The amounts distributed shall be apportioned and distributed to the counties and cities as provided in section 30(a) of this article, to be used for highway purposes.

4. The moneys apportioned or distributed under this section to the state road fund, the state transportation fund, the state road bond fund, counties, cities, towns or villages shall not be included within the definition of "total state revenues" as that term is used in section 17 of Article X of this constitution nor be considered as an "expense of state government" as that term is used in section 20 of article X of this constitution.

Section 30(C). Transportation Programs and Facilities, Administration of by Commission, Use of Moneys

The highways and transportation commission shall have authority to plan, locate, relocate, establish, acquire, construct, maintain, control, and as provided by law to operate, develop and fund public transportation facilities as part of any state transportation system or program such as but not limited to aviation, mass transportation, transportation of elderly and handicapped, railroads, ports, waterborne commerce and intermodal connections, provided that funds other than those designated or dedicated for highway purposes in or deposited in the state road fund or the state road bond fund pursuant to sections 30(a) or 30(b) of this constitution are made available for such purposes. No moneys which are distributed to the state transportation fund pursuant to section 30(b) shall be used for any purpose other than for transportation purposes as provided in this section.

Section 30(D). Prohibition Against Diverting Revenue for Non-Highway Purposes—Severability of Provisions—Effective Date

1. No state revenues derived from highway users which are to be allocated, distributed or deposited in the state road fund pursuant to either section 30(a) or section 30(b) shall be diverted from the highway purposes and uses specified in subsection 1 of section 30(b). No state revenues derived from highway users which are to be allocated, distributed or deposited in the state road bond fund pursuant to subdivision (3) of subsection 2 of section 30(b) shall be diverted from the highway purposes and uses specified in said subdivision (3).

2. All of the provisions of sections 29, 30(a), 30(b), 30(c) and 30(d) shall be self executing. All of the provisions of sections 29, 30(a), 30(b), 30(c) and 30(d) are severable. If any provision of sections 29, 30(a), 30(b), 30(c) and 30(d) is found by a court of competent jurisdiction to be unconstitutional or unconstitutionally enacted, the remaining provisions of these sections shall be and remain valid.

3. The provisions of sections 29, 30(a), 30(b), 30(c) and 30(d) shall become effective on July 1, 2005.

Section 31. State Highways in Municipalities

Any state highway authorized herein to be located in any municipality may be constructed without limitations concerning the distance between houses or other buildings abutting such highway or concerning the width or type of construction. The commission may enter into contracts with cities, counties or other political subdivisions for and concerning the maintenance of, and regulation of traffic on any state highway within such cities, counties or subdivision.

Section 32. Apportionment of Funds for Supplementary State Highways

The funds which are allotted by the commission to the construction or acquisition of supplementary state highways and bridges in each of the counties of the state shall be apportioned to the several counties as follows: One-fourth in the ratio that the area of each county bears to the area of the state, one-fourth in the ratio of the population, and two-fourths on such basis as the commission may deem to be for the best interest of highway users; provided the areas and population of cities having a population of 150,000 or more shall not be considered in making such apportionment, and the latest available United States decennial census shall be used; provided further, that if traffic on any supplementary state highway becomes such that a higher type than ordinary supplementary highway construction shall be required, then the commission may construct such higher type and charge such extra cost to unallotted state highway funds. Supplementary state highways shall be selected by mutual agreement of the commission and the local officials having charge of or jurisdiction over roads in the territory through which such supplementary state highways are to be constructed.

Section 33. Retirement Benefits Not Changed

Any transfer of employees made pursuant to the provisions of this article shall not affect or abridge any rights or benefits accrued under any retirement system in which such employees are members on the effective date of this article, and the employees may continue coverage under such retirement system until otherwise provided by law.

Section 34. Recognition of Outstanding Bonds—Determination, Certification and Collection of Annual State Highway Bond Tax

All bonds issued under or recognized by section 44a of article IV of the previous constitution, which remain unpaid shall be valid obligations of the state and shall be paid according to the tenor thereof. On or before the first day of July of each year the state auditor shall determine the rate of taxation for that year necessary to raise the amount of money needed to pay the principal and interest maturing in the next succeeding year, taking into consideration available funds, delinquencies and the cost of collection. The auditor shall annually certify the rate of taxation so determined to the officer in each county whose duty it is to make up and certify the tax books wherein are extended the state taxes. Said officers shall extend upon the tax books the taxes to be collected and certify the same to the collector of revenue of their respective counties, who shall collect such taxes at the same time and in the same manner and by the same means as are provided by law for the collection of state and county taxes, and pay the same into the state treasury

AGRICULTURE

Section 35. Agriculture, Department of—Director, How Appointed—Funds to be Provided, How

The department of agriculture shall be in charge of a director appointed by the governor by and with the advice and consent of the senate. The general assembly shall provide the department of agriculture with funds adequate for administration of its functions; and shall enact such laws and provide such other appropriations as may be required to protect, foster and develop the agricultural resources of the state.

Section 36. Forestry and Forest Fires

The general assembly may enact laws to encourage forestry, and prevent and suppress forest fires on private lands.

ECONOMIC DEVELOPMENT

Section 36(A). Economic Development, Department of— Duties of De Part Ment— Director, How Appointed

The department of economic development shall be in charge of a director appointed by the governor, by and with the advice and consent of the senate. The department shall administer all programs provided by law relating to the promotion of the economy of the state, the economic development of the state, trade and business, and other activities and programs impacting on the economy of the state.

INSURANCE

Section 36(B). Department of Insurance, Established— Director, Appointment— Office of Consumer Affairs to be Established Within Department, Duties

The department of insurance shall be headed by a director of the department of insurance who shall be appointed by the governor with the advice and consent of the senate. The organization and duties of the department of insurance shall be determined by law. All references to the division of insurance and the insurance division in this constitution and in the statutes shall mean the department of insurance. There shall be an office of consumer affairs within the department of insurance to investigate in conjunction with other personnel of the department all allegations of unfair or unlawful acts by any person or entity whose activities are regulated by the department of insurance.

SOCIAL SERVICES

Section 37. Social services, department of—duties of department —director, how appointed.—The health and general welfare of the people are matters of primary public concern; and to secure them there shall be established a department of social services in charge of a director appointed by the governor, by and with the advice and consent of the senate, charged with promoting improved health and other social services to the citizens of the state as provided by law, and the general assembly may grant power with respect thereto to counties, cities or other political subdivisions of the state.

MENTAL HEALTH

Section 37(A). Mental Health, Department of—Duties of Department—Director, How Appointed

The department of mental health shall be in charge of a director who shall be appointed by the commission, as provided by law, and by and with the advice and consent of the senate. The department shall provide treatment, care, education and training for persons suffering from mental illness or retardation, shall have administrative control of the state hospitals and other institutions and centers established for these purposes and shall administer such other programs as provided by law.

Section 39. Cooperation With Federal and Other State Governments

in all matters of public welfare the general assembly may provide by law for cooperation with the United States, or other states.

CONSERVATION

Section 40(A). Conservation Commission, Members, Qualifications, Terms, How Appointed—Duties of Commission—Expenses of Members

The control, management, restoration, conservation and regulation of the bird, fish, game, forestry and all wildlife resources of the state, including hatcheries, sanctuaries, refuges, reservations and all other property owned, acquired or used for such purposes and the acquisition and establishment thereof, and the administration of all laws pertaining thereto, shall be vested in a conservation commission consisting of four members appointed by the governor, by and with the advice and consent of the senate, not more than two of whom shall be of the same political party. The members shall have knowledge of and interest in wildlife conservation. The members shall hold office for terms of six years beginning on the first day of July of consecutive odd years. Two of the terms shall be concurrent; one shall begin two years before and one two years after the concurrent terms. If the governor fails to fill a vacancy within thirty days, the remaining members shall fill the vacancy for the unexpired term. The members shall receive no salary or other compensation for their services as members, but shall receive their necessary traveling and other expenses incurred while actually engaged in the discharge of their official duties.

Section 40(B). Incumbent Members

The members of the present conservation commission shall serve out the terms for which they were appointed, with all their powers and duties. Section 41. Acquisition of property—eminent domain.—The commission may acquire by purchase, gift, eminent domain, or otherwise, all property necessary, useful or convenient for its purposes, and shall exercise the right of eminent domain as provided by law for the highway commission.

Section 42. Director of Conservation and Personnel of Commission

The commission shall appoint a director of conservation who, with its approval, shall appoint the assistants and other employees deemed necessary by the commission. The commission shall fix the qualifications and salaries of the director and all appointees and employees, and none of its members shall be an appointee or employee.

Section 43(A). Sales Tax, Use for Conservation Purposes

for the purpose of providing additional moneys to be expended and used by the conservation commission, department of conservation, for the control, management, restoration, conservation and regulation of the bird, fish, game, forestry and wildlife resources of the state, including the purchase or other acquisition of property for said purposes, and for the administration of the laws pertaining thereto, an additional sales tax of one-eighth of one percent is hereby levied and imposed upon all sellers for the privilege of selling tangible personal property or rendering taxable services at retail in this state upon the sales and services which now are or hereafter are listed and set forth in, and, except as to the amount of tax, subject to the provisions of and to be collected as provided in the "Sales Tax Law" and subject to the rules and regulations promulgated in connection therewith; and an additional use tax of one-eighth of one percent is levied and imposed for the privilege of storing, using or consuming within this state any article of tangible personal property as set forth and provided in the "Compensating Use Tax Law" and, except as to the amount of the tax, subject to the provisions of and to be collected as provided in the "Compensating Use Tax Law" and subject to the rules and regulations promulgated in connection therewith.

Section 43(B). Use of Revenue and Funds of Conservation Commission

The moneys arising from the additional sales and use taxes provided for in section 43(a) hereof and all fees, moneys or funds arising from the operation and transactions of the conservation commission, department of conservation, and from the application and the administration of the laws and regulations pertaining to the bird, fish, game, forestry and wildlife resources of the state and from the sale of property used for said purposes, shall be expended and used by the conservation commission, department of conservation, for the control, management, restoration, conservation and regulation of the bird, fish, game, forestry and wildlife resources of the state, including the purchase or other acquisition of property for said purposes, and for the administration of the laws pertaining thereto, and for no other purpose. The moneys and funds of the conservation commission arising from the additional sales and use taxes provided for in 43(a) hereof shall also be used by the conservation commission, department of conservation, to make payments to counties for the unimproved value of land for distribution to the appropriate political subdivisions as payment in lieu of real property taxes for privately owned land acquired by the commission after July 1, 1977 and for land classified as forest cropland in the forest cropland program administered by the department of conservation in such amounts as may be determined by the conservation commission, but in no event shall the amount determined be less than the property tax being paid at the time of purchase of acquired lands.

Section 43(C). Effective Date—Self-Enforceability

The effective date of this amendment* shall be July 1, 1977. All laws inconsistent with this amendment shall no longer remain in full force and effect after July 1, 1977. All of the provisions of sections 43(a)-(c) shall be self-enforcing except that the general assembly shall adjust brackets for the collection of the sales and use taxes.

Section 44. Self-Enforceability—Enabling Clause—Repealing Clause

Sections 40-43, inclusive, of this article shall be self-enforcing, and laws not inconsistent therewith may be enacted in aid thereof. All existing laws inconsistent with this article shall no longer remain in force or effect.

Section 45. Rules and Regulations—Filing—Review

The rules and regulations of the commission not relating to its organization and internal management shall become effective not less than ten days after being filed with the secretary of state as provided in section 16 of this article, and such final rules and regulations affecting private rights as are judicial or quasi-judicial in nature shall be subject to the judicial review provided in section 22 of article V.

Section 46. Distribution of Rules and Regulations

The commission shall supply to all persons on request, printed copies of its rules and regulations not relating to organization or internal management.

NATURAL RESOURCES

Section 47. Natural Resources, Department of—Duties of Department—Director, How Appointed

The department of natural resources shall be in charge of a director appointed by the governor, by and with the advice and consent of the senate. The department shall administer the programs of the state as provided by law relating to environmental control and the conservation and management of natural resources.

Section 47(A). Sales and Use Tax Levied for Soil and Water Conservation and for State Parks—Distribution of Parks Sales Tax Fund to Counties, Purpose, Limitation

for the purpose of providing additional monies to be expended and used by the department of natural resources through the state soil and water districts commission as defined in Section 278.070, RSMo, for the saving of the soil and water of this state for the conservation of the productive power of Missouri agricultural land, and by the department of natural resources through the division responsible for the State park system for the acquisition, development, maintenance and operation of state parks and state historic sites in accordance with Chapter 253, RSMo, and for the administration of the laws pertaining thereto, an additional sales tax of one-tenth of one percent is hereby levied and imposed upon all sellers for the privilege of selling tangible personal property or rendering taxable services at retail in this state upon the sales and services which now are or hereafter are listed and set forth in, and, except as to the amount of tax, subject to the provisions of and to be collected as provided in the "Sales Tax Law" and subject to the rules and regulations promulgated in connection therewith; and an additional use tax of one-tenth of one percent is levied and imposed for the privilege of storing, using or consuming within this state any article of tangible personal property as set forth and provided in the "Compensating Use Tax Law" and, except as to the amount of the tax, subject to the provisions of and to be collected as provided in the "Compensating Use Tax Law" and subject to the rules and regulations promulgated in connection therewith. in addition, monies deposited in the state parks sales tax fund pursuant to the provisions of section 47(b) of this article shall also be appropriated to make payments to counties for a period of five years for the unimproved value of land for distribution to the appropriate political subdivisions as payment in lieu of real property taxes for privately owned land acquired by the department of natural resources for park purposes after July 1, 1985, in such amounts as determined by appropriation, but in no event shall such amounts be more than the amount of property tax imposed by political subdivisions at the time the department acquired or acquires such land.

Section 47(B). Disbursement of Revenue, Purposes

Fifty percent of the monies arising from the additional sales and use taxes provided for in Section 47(a) hereof shall be deposited in the Soil and Water Sales Tax Fund and fifty percent shall be deposited in the State Park Sales Tax Fund, and the monies in both funds shall be expended pursuant to appropriation by the General Assembly and used by the state soil and water districts commission and the department of natural resources for the purposes set forth in Section 47(a), and for no other purpose.

Section 47(C). Provisions Self-Enforcing, Exception—Not Part of General Revenue Or Expense of State—Effective and Expiration Dates

All laws inconsistent with this amendment shall no longer remain in full force and effect after the effective date of this section. All of the provisions of Sections 47(a), 47(b) and 47(c) shall be self-enforcing except that the General Assembly shall adjust brackets for the collection of the sales and use taxes. The additional revenue provided by Sections 47(a), 47(b) and 47(c) shall not be part of the "total state revenue" within the meaning of Sections 17 and 18 of Article X of this Constitution. The expenditure of this additional revenue shall not be an "expense of state government" under Section 20 of Article X of this Constitution. Upon voter approval of this measure in a general election held in 2006, or at a special election to be called by the governor for that purpose, the provisions of this section, 47(b), and 47(a) shall be reauthorized and continue until a general election is held in 2016 or at a special election to be called by the governor for that purpose. Every ten years thereafter, the issue of whether to continue to impose the sales and use tax described in this section shall be resubmitted to the voters for approval. If a majority of the voters fail to approve the continuance of such sales and use tax, Section 47(a), 47(b), and 47(c) shall terminate at the end of the second fiscal year after the last election was held.

PUBLIC SAFETY

Section 48. Public Safety, Department of—Duties of Department—Director, How Appointed

The department of public safety shall be in charge of a director to be appointed by the governor by and with the advice and consent of the senate, and shall administer the programs provided by law to protect and safeguard the lives and property of the people of the state.

LABOR AND INDUSTRIAL RELATIONS

Section 49. Labor and Industrial Relations, Department of—Duties—Commission Members, How Appointed, Terms, Qualifications

The department of labor and industrial relations shall be in charge of a "Labor and Industrial Relations Commission" consisting of three members appointed by the governor by and with the advice and consent of the senate. One member of the commission shall be a person who, on account of his previous vocation, employment, affiliation or interests shall be classified as a representative of employers, and one member who, on account of his previous vocation, employment, affiliation or interests shall be classified as a representative of employees, and one member, who, by reason of his previous activities and interests shall be classified as a representative of the public and who is licensed to practice law in the state of Missouri; except that not more than two members of the commission shall be of the same political party. A member of the commission shall be designated by the governor as the chairman. The labor and industrial commission shall be the successor to the industrial commission and the terms of members shall be as provided by law for the industrial commission. The department shall also administer the programs of the state relating to the protection and improvement of human rights.

OFFICE OF ADMINISTRATION

Section 50. Administration, Office of—Commissioner, How Appointed

The office of administration shall be in charge of a commissioner of administration. The commissioner shall be appointed by the governor by and with the advice and consent of the senate.

APPOINTMENT OF ADMINISTRATIVE HEADS

Section 51. Appointments, How Made—Failure to Confirm, Effect of

The appointment of all members of administrative boards and commissions and of all department and division heads, as provided by law, shall be made by the governor. All members of administrative boards and commissions, all department and division heads and all other officials appointed by the governor shall be made only by and with the advice and consent of the senate. The authority to act of any person whose appointment requires the advice and consent of the senate shall commence, if the senate is in session, upon receiving the advice and consent of the senate. If the senate is not in session, the authority to act shall commence immediately upon appointment by the governor but shall terminate if the advice and consent of the senate is not given within thirty days after the senate has convened in regular or special session. If the senate fails to give its advice and consent to any appointee, that person shall not be reappointed by the governor to the same office or position.

HIGHER EDUCATION

Section 52. Higher Education, Department of Established—Coordinating Board for Higher Education Established, Members, Terms, Qualifications

There shall be established a department of higher education. A "Coordinating Board for Higher Education" which shall consist of nine members appointed by the governor by and with the advice and consent of the senate shall be established within the department. The qualifications and terms of the members of the board shall be fixed by law, but not more than five of its members shall be of the same political party. The coordinating board shall succeed the commission on higher education with all its powers and duties and shall have such other powers and duties as may be prescribed by law.

NONDISCRIMINATION IN APPOINTMENTS

Section 53. Discrimination As to Race, Creed, Color Or National Origin Prohibited

The appointment of all members of administrative boards and commissions and of all departments and division heads and all the employees thereof shall be made without regard to race, creed, color or national origin.

ARTICLE V: JUDICIAL DEPARTMENT

Section 1. Judicial Power—Constitutional Courts

The judicial power of the state shall be vested in a supreme court, a court of appeals consisting of districts as prescribed by law, and circuit courts.

Section 2. Supreme Court—Controlling Decisions—Number of Judges—Sessions

The supreme court shall be the highest court in the state. Its jurisdiction shall be coextensive with the state. Its decisions shall be controlling in all other courts. It shall be composed of seven judges, who shall hold their sessions in Jefferson City at times fixed by the court.

Section 3. Jurisdiction of The Supreme Court

The supreme court shall have exclusive appellate jurisdiction in all cases involving the validity of a treaty or statute of the United States, or of a statute or provision of the constitution of this state, the construction of the revenue laws of this state, the title to any state office and in all cases where the punishment imposed is death. The court of appeals shall have general appellate jurisdiction in all cases except those within the exclusive jurisdiction of the supreme court.

Section 4. Superior Courts to Control Inferior Courts—Courts Administrator, Salary—Reapportionment Commission, Appointment

1. The supreme court shall have general superintending control over all courts and tribunals. Each district of the court of appeals shall have general superintending control over all courts and tribunals in its jurisdiction. The supreme court and districts of the court of appeals may issue and determine original remedial writs. Supervisory authority over all courts is vested in the supreme court which may make appropriate delegations of this power.

2. The supreme court may appoint a state courts administrator and other staff to aid in the administration of the courts, and it shall appoint a clerk of the supreme court and may appoint other staff to aid in the administration of the business of the supreme court. Each such appointee shall serve at the pleasure of the court. The clerk's and administrator's salary shall be fixed by law. All other appointees shall have salaries fixed by the court within the legislative limits of the appropriation made for that purpose.

3. in the event that six commissioners of the supreme court are not available to sit as a reapportionment commission as provided in sections 2, 3 and 7 of article III of the constitution of this state, a commission composed of six members appointed by the supreme court from among the judges of the court of appeals, shall serve in lieu of the commissioners of the supreme court. No more than two members of any division of the court of appeals shall be appointed to the commission.

Section 5. Rules of Practice and Procedure—Duty of Supreme Court—Power of Legislature

The supreme court may establish rules relating to practice, procedure and pleading for all courts and administrative tribunals, which shall have the force and effect of law. The rules shall not change substantive rights, or the law relating to evidence, the oral examination of witnesses, juries, the right of trial by jury, or the right of appeal. The court shall publish the rules and fix the day on which they take effect, but no rule shall take effect before six months after its publication. Any rule may be annulled or amended in whole or in part by a law limited to the purpose.

Section 6. Assignment of Judges—Authority of Supreme Court—Eligible Judges

The supreme court may make temporary transfers of judicial personnel from one court or district to another as the administration of justice requires, and may establish rules with respect thereto. Any judge shall be eligible to sit temporarily on any court upon assignment by the supreme court or pursuant to supreme court rule.

Section 7. Supreme Court and Court of Appeals May Sit in Divisions

The supreme court may sit en banc or in divisions as the court may determine. Any district of the court of appeals may sit at such places within the district and in divisions as the judges of such district may determine. Each division of the supreme court or of the court of appeals shall be composed of not less than three judges, at least one of whom shall be a regular judge of the court. A majority of a division shall constitute a quorum thereof, and all orders, judgments, and decrees of a division, as to causes and matters pending before it, shall have the force and effect of those of the court.

Section 8. Chief Justice and Chief Judges, Election, Terms —Authority of Chief Justice

The judges of the supreme court shall elect from their number a chief justice to preside over the court en banc, and the judges of the court of appeals in each district shall elect from their number a chief judge of the district. The terms of the chief justice and chief judges shall be fixed by the courts over which they preside. The chief justice of the supreme court shall be the chief administrative officer of the judicial system and, subject to the supervisory authority of the supreme court, shall supervise the administration of the courts of this state.

Section 9. Transfer of Causes to Supreme Court En Banc

A cause in the supreme court shall be transferred to the court en banc when the members of a division are equally divided in opinion, or when the division shall so order, or on application of the losing party when a member of the division dissents from the opinion therein, or pursuant to supreme court rule.

Section 10. Transfer of Cases From Court of Appeals to Supreme Court— Scope of Review

Cases pending in the court of appeals shall be transferred to the supreme court when any participating judge dissents from the majority opinion and certifies that he deems said opinion to be contrary to any previous decision of the supreme court or of the court of appeals, or any district of the court of appeals. Cases pending in the court of appeals may be transferred to the supreme court by order of the majority of the judges of the participating district of the court of appeals, after opinion, or by order of the supreme court before or after opinion because of the general interest or importance of a question involved in the case, or for the purpose of reexamining the existing law, or pursuant to supreme court rule. The supreme court may finally determine all causes coming to it from the court of appeals, whether by certification, transfer or certiorari, the same as on original appeal.

Section 11. Want of Jurisdiction, Effect—Transfers

in all proceedings reviewable on appeal by the supreme court or the court of appeals, appeals shall go directly to the court or district having jurisdiction, but want of jurisdiction shall not be ground for dismissal, and the proceeding shall be transferred to the appellate court having jurisdiction. An original action filed in a court lacking jurisdiction or venue shall be transferred to the appropriate court.

Section 12. Judicial Opinions—Filing and Publication—Memorandum Decisions and Orders

The opinions of the supreme court and court of appeals and all divisions or districts of said courts shall be in writing and filed in the respective causes, and shall become a part of the records of the court, be available for publication, and shall be public records. The supreme court and the court of appeals may issue memorandum decisions or dispose of a cause by order pursuant to and as authorized by supreme court rule.

Section 13. Court of Appeals, Districts, Judges

The court of appeals shall be organized into separate districts, the number, not less than three, geographical boundaries, and territorial jurisdiction of which shall be prescribed by law. Each district of the court of appeals shall be composed of such number of judges, not less than three, as may be provided by law.

Section 14. Circuit Courts—Jurisdiction—Sessions

(a) The circuit courts shall have original jurisdiction over all cases and matters, civil and criminal. Such courts may issue and determine original remedial writs and shall sit at times and places within the circuit as determined by the circuit court.

(b) Procedures for the adjudication of small claims shall be as provided by law.

Section 15. Judicial Circuits—Establishment and Changes—General Terms and Divisions—Judges—Presiding Judge—Court Personnel

1. The state shall be divided into convenient circuits of contiguous counties. in each circuit there shall be at least one circuit judge. The circuits may be changed or abolished by law as public convenience and the administration of justice may require, but no judge shall be removed from office during his term by reason of alteration of the geographical boundaries of a circuit. Any circuit or associate circuit judge may temporarily sit in any other circuit at the request of a judge thereof. in circuits having more than one judge, the court may sit in general term or in divisions. The circuit judges of the circuit may make rules for the circuit not inconsistent with the rules of the supreme court.

2. Each circuit shall have such number of circuit judges as provided by law.

3. The circuit and associate circuit judges in each circuit shall select by secret ballot a circuit judge from their number to serve as presiding judge. The presiding judge shall have general administrative authority over the court and its divisions. 4. Personnel to aid in the business of the circuit court shall be selected as provided by law or in accordance with a governmental charter of a political subdivision of this state. Where there is a separate probate division of the circuit court, the judge of the probate division shall, until otherwise provided by law, appoint a clerk and other nonjudicial personnel for the probate division.

Section 16. Associate Circuit Judges, Selection

Each county shall have such number of associate circuit judges as provided by law. There shall be at least one resident associate circuit judge in each county. Associate circuit judges shall be selected or elected in each county. in those circuits where the circuit judge is selected under section 25 of article 5 of the constitution the associate circuit judge shall be selected in the same manner. All other associate circuit judges shall be elected in the county in which they are to serve.

Section 17. Associate Circuit Judges, Jurisdiction

Associate circuit judges may hear and determine all cases, civil or criminal and all other matters as now provided by law for magistrate or probate judges and may be assigned such additional cases or classes of cases as may be provided by law. in probate matters the associate circuit judge shall have general equitable jurisdiction.

Section 18. Judicial Review of Action of Administrative Agencies—Scope of Review

All final decisions, findings, rules and orders on any administrative officer or body existing under the constitution or by law, which are judicial or quasi-judicial and affect private rights, shall be subject to direct review by the courts as provided by law; and such review shall include the determination whether the same are authorized by law, and in cases in which a hearing is required by law, whether the same are supported by competent and substantial evidence upon the whole record. Unless otherwise provided by law, administrative decisions, findings, rules and orders subject to review under this section or which are otherwise subject to direct judicial review, shall be reviewed in such manner and by such court as the supreme court by rule shall direct and the court so designated shall, in addition to its other jurisdiction, have jurisdiction to hear and determine any such review proceeding.

Section 19. Terms of Judges

Judges of the supreme court and of the court of appeals shall be selected for terms of twelve years, judges of the circuit courts for terms of six years, and associate circuit judges for terms of four years.

Section 20. Salaries and Compensation of Judges—Provision Against Other Special Compensation and Practice of Law—Travel and Other Expenses

All judges shall receive as salary the total amount of their present compensation until otherwise provided by law, but no judge's salary shall be diminished during his term of office. No judge shall receive any other or additional compensation for any public service. No supreme, appellate, circuit or associate circuit judge shall practice law or do law business. Judges may receive reasonable traveling and other expenses allowed by law.

Section 21. Judges—Qualifications—Age Requirements—License to Practice Law

Judges of the supreme court and of the court of appeals shall have been citizens of the United States for at least fifteen years, and qualified voters of the state for nine years next preceding their selection. Such judges shall be at least thirty years of age. Except as provided by section 6, judges of the court of appeals shall be residents of the court of appeals district in which they serve. Circuit judges shall have been citizens of the United States for at least ten years, and qualified voters of this state three years next preceding their selection, and be not less than thirty years of age and residents of the circuit for at least one year. Associate circuit judges shall be qualified voters of this state and residents of the county, at least twenty-five years old, and have such other qualifications as may be provided by law. Every supreme, appellate, circuit, and associate circuit court judge shall be licensed to practice law in this state.

Section 22. Court of Appeals Clerks and Personnel—Salaries

Each district of the court of appeals shall appoint a clerk of the court and other personnel to aid in the administration of the business of the court. Their salaries shall be within the limit of the legislative appropriation for that purpose.

Section 23. Municipal Judges and Court Personnel—Selection—Terms—Compensation—Jurisdiction—Appeals—Role of Associate Circuit Judges

Each circuit may have such municipal judges as provided by law and the necessary non-judicial personnel assisting them. The selection, tenure and compensation of such judges and such personnel shall be as provided by law, or in cities having a charter form of government as provided by such charter. A municipal judge may be a part-time judge except where prohibited by ordinance or charter of the municipality. A municipal judge shall hear and determine violations of municipal ordinances in one or more municipalities. Until otherwise provided by law, or supreme court rule, the practice, procedure, right to and method of appeal before and from municipal judges shall be as heretofore provided with respect to municipal courts. Associate circuit judges shall hear and determine violations of municipal ordinances in any municipality with a population of under four hundred thousand within the circuit for which a municipal judge is not provided, or upon request of the governing body of any municipality with a population of under four hundred thousand within the circuit.

Section 24. Retirement, Removal and Discipline of Judges, Commission On— Composition, Terms, Duties, Procedures, Reimbursement of Expenses—Additional Duties Prohibited

1. There shall be a commission on retirement, removal, and discipline, composed of two citizens who are not members of the bar, appointed by the governor, two lawyers appointed by the board of governors of The Missouri Bar, one judge of the court of appeals to be selected by a majority of the judges of the court of appeals, and one judge of the circuit courts to be selected by a majority of the circuit judges of this state. The commission shall receive and investigate all requests and suggestions for retirement for disability, and all complaints concerning misconduct of all judges, members of the judicial commissions, and of this commission. No member of the commission shall participate in any matter in which he has a personal interest. If a member is disqualified to participate in any matter before the commission, the respective selecting authority shall select a substitute to sit during such disqualification. of the members first appointed, each of the citizen members shall be appointed for a term of two years and each of the lawyer members for a term of four years, and each of the judge members for a term of six years; and thereafter members shall be appointed for a term of six years.

2. Upon recommendation by an affirmative vote of at least four members of the commission, the supreme court en banc shall retire from office any judge or any member of any judicial commission or any member of this commission who is found to be unable to discharge the duties of his office with efficiency because of permanent sickness or physical or mental infirmity. A judge, except a municipal judge so retired shall receive one-half of his regular compensation during the remainder of his term of office. Where a judge subject to retirement under other provisions of law, has been retired under the provisions of this section, the time during which he was retired for disability under this section shall count as time served for purposes of retirement under other provisions of this constitution or of law.

3. Upon recommendation by an affirmative vote of at least four members of the commission, the supreme court en banc, upon concurring with such recommendation, shall remove, suspend, discipline or reprimand any judge of any court or any member of any judicial commission or of this commission, for the commission of a crime, or for misconduct, habitual drunkenness, willful neglect of duty, corruption in office, incompetency or any offense involving moral turpitude, or oppression in office. No action taken under this section shall be a bar to or prevent any other action authorized by law.

4. A judge is disqualified from acting as a judicial officer while there is pending an indictment or information charging him in any court in the United States with a crime punishable as a felony under the laws of Missouri or the United States, or a recommendation to the supreme court by the commission for his removal, or retirement, or after articles of impeachment have been voted by the house of representatives. A judge so disqualified shall continue to receive his salary.

5. On recommendation of the commission, the supreme court shall suspend a judge from office without salary when in any court in the United States he pleads guilty or no contest to, or is found guilty of, an offense punishable as a felony under the laws of Missouri or the United States, or of any other offense that involves moral turpitude. If he is suspended and his conviction becomes final the supreme court shall remove him from office. If his conviction is reversed and he is discharged from that charge by order of court or of the prosecuting officer, whether without further trial or after further trial and a finding of not guilty, his suspension terminates and he shall be paid his salary for the period of suspension.

6. Recommendations to the supreme court by the commission shall be made only after notice and hearing. Rules for the administration of this section and for the procedures thereunder shall be prescribed by supreme court rule unless otherwise provided by law.

7. Members of the commission shall be reimbursed for their actual and necessary expenses incurred in the performance of their duties.

8. Additional duties shall not be imposed by law or supreme court rule upon the commission on retirement, removal and discipline.

Section 25(A). Nonpartisan Selection of Judges—Courts Subject to Plan— Appointments to Fill Vacancies

Whenever a vacancy shall occur in the office of judge of any of the following courts of this state, to wit: The supreme court, the court of appeals, or in the office of circuit or associate circuit judge within the city of St. Louis and Jackson county, the governor shall fill such vacancy by appointing one of three persons possessing the qualifications for such office, who shall be nominated and whose names shall be submitted to the governor by a nonpartisan judicial commission established and organized as hereinafter provided. If the governor fails to appoint any of the nominees within sixty days after the list of nominees is submitted, the nonpartisan judicial commission making the nomination shall appoint one of the nominees to fill the vacancy.

Section 25(B). Adoption of Plan in Other Circuits— Petitions and Elections— Form of Petition Ballots

At any general election the qualified voters of any judicial circuit outside of the city of St. Louis and Jackson county, may by a majority of those voting on the question elect to have the circuit and associate circuit judges appointed by the governor in the manner provided for the appointment of judges to the courts designated in section 25(a), or, outside the city of St. Louis and Jackson county, to discontinue any such plan. The question of whether the circuit and associate circuit judges of any such circuit shall be so appointed shall be submitted to the voters of each county in any circuit at the next general election whenever petitions therefor signed by ten percent of the legal voters of each county in the circuit voting for the office of governor at the last election thereof are filed in the office of secretary of state at least 90 days before such election. The question shall be presented as follows:

"Shall the circuit and associate circuit judges of the . . . . judicial circuit be selected as provided in Section 25 of Article V of the Missouri Constitution? Yes ¨ No ¨ (Mark One)".

The provisions of law with respect to initiative petitions shall apply insofar as applicable relative to the certification of the petitions to local officials by the secretary of state, the preparation, printing, publishing and distribution of the judicial ballots required by this section, the holding and conduct of the election, and the counting, canvassing, return, certification, and proclamation of the votes. If a majority of the votes upon the question are cast in favor of the adoption in each county comprising the circuit, the nonpartisan selection of the circuit and associate judges shall be adopted in the circuit. The question of selection of circuit and associate circuit judges in the manner provided in section 25(a) shall not be submitted more often than once every four years. If any judicial circuit adopts the nonpartisan selection of the circuit and associate circuit judges under the provisions of this section, the question of its discontinuance shall not be submitted more often than once every four years and may be submitted at any general election and shall be proceeded upon insofar as may be applicable in like manner as prescribed in this section for the original adoption of the plan. The petition shall be in substantially the following form:

to the Honorable Officials in general charge of elections for the county of . . . . for the state of Missouri: We, the undersigned, legal voters of the state of Missouri, and of the county of . . . ., respectfully demand that the question of the discontinuance of the nonpartisan selection of the circuit and associate circuit judges be submitted to the legal voters of the . . . . judicial circuit, for their approval or rejection, at the general election to be held on the . . . day of . . . . . , A.D. 19. . . .

The ballot shall provide as follows:

"Shall the nonpartisan appointment by the governor of the circuit and associate circuit judges be discontinued in the . . . . judicial circuit? ¨ Yes ¨ No (Place an "X" in one square.)"

If a majority of the votes upon the question are cast in favor of such discontinuance in each county comprising the circuit, the nonpartisan selection of the circuit and associate circuit judges shall be discontinued in such judicial circuit. If the nonpartisan selection of the judges be discontinued in any such judicial circuit, other than the city of St. Louis and Jackson county, the selection of such judges therein shall be made as otherwise prescribed by law. This section shall be self-enforcing.

Section 25(C)(1). Tenure of Judges—Declaration of Candidacy—Form of Judicial Ballot—Rejection and Retention

Each judge appointed pursuant to the provisions of sections 25(a)–(g) shall hold office for a term ending December thirty-first following the next general election after the expiration of twelve months in the office. Any judge holding office, or elected thereto, at the time of the election by which the provisions of sections 25(a)–(g) become applicable to his office, shall, unless removed for cause, remain in office for the term to which he would have been entitled had the provisions of sections 25(a)–(g) not become applicable to his office. Not less than sixty days prior to the holding of the general election next preceding the expiration of his term of office, any judge whose office is subject to the provisions of sections 25(a)–(g) may file in the office of the secretary of state a declaration of candidacy for election to succeed himself. If a declaration is not so filed by any judge, the vacancy resulting from the expiration of his term of office shall be filled by appointment as herein provided. If such declaration is filed, his name shall be submitted at said next general election to the voters eligible to vote within the state if his office is that of judge of the supreme court, or within the geographic jurisdiction limit of the district where he serves if his office is that of a judge of the court of appeals, or within the circuit if his office is that of circuit judge, or within the county if his office is that of associate circuit judge on a separate judicial ballot, without party designation, reading:

"Shall Judge. . . . .(Here the name of the judge shall be inserted) of the. . . . . (Here the title of the court shall be inserted) be retained in office? Yes ¨ No ¨ (Mark an "X" in the box you prefer.)"

If a majority of those voting on the question vote against retaining him in office, upon the expiration of his term of office, a vacancy shall exist which shall be filled by appointment as provided in section 25(a); otherwise, said judge shall, unless removed for cause, remain in office for the number of years after December thirty-first following such election as is provided for the full term of such office, and at the expiration of each such term shall be eligible for retention in office by election in the manner here prescribed.

Section 25(C)(2). Certification of Names Upon Declaration—Law Applicable to Elections

Whenever a declaration of candidacy for election to succeed himself is filed by any judge or associate circuit judge under the provisions of this section, the secretary of state shall not less than thirty days before the election certify the name of said judge or associate circuit judge and the official title of his office to the clerks of the county courts, and to the boards of election commissioners in counties or cities having such boards, or to such other officials as may hereafter be provided by law, of all counties and cities wherein the question of retention of such judge in office is to be submitted to the voters, and, until legislation shall be expressly provided otherwise therefor, the judicial ballots required by this section shall be prepared, printed, published and distributed, and the election upon the question of retention of such judge in office shall be conducted and the votes counted, canvassed, returned, certified and proclaimed by such public officials in such manner as is now provided by the statutory law governing voting upon measures proposed by the initiative.

Section 25(D). Nonpartisan Judicial Commissions—Number, Qualifications, Selection and Terms of Members—Majority Rule—Reimbursement of Expenses— Rules of Supreme Court

Nonpartisan judicial commissions whose duty it shall be to nominate and submit to the governor names of persons for appointment as provided by sections 25(a)–(g) are hereby established and shall be organized on the following basis: for vacancies in the office of judge of the supreme court or of the court of appeals, there shall be one such commission, to be known as "The Appellate Judicial Commission"; for vacancies in the office of circuit judge or associate circuit judge of any circuit court subject to the provisions of sections 25(a)–(g) there shall be one such commission, to be known as "The . . . Circuit Judicial Commission", for each judicial circuit which shall be subject to the provisions of sections 25(a)–(g); the appellate judicial commission shall consist of a judge of the supreme court selected by the members of the supreme court, and the remaining members shall be chosen in the following manner: The members of the bar of this state residing in each court of appeals district shall elect one of their number to serve as a member of said commission, and the governor shall appoint one citizen, not a member of the bar, from among the residents of each court of appeals district, to serve as a member of said commission, and the members of the commission shall select one of their number to serve as chairman. Each circuit judicial commission shall consist of five members, one of whom shall be the chief judge of the district of the court of appeals within which the judicial circuit of such commission, or the major portion of the population of said circuit is situated and the remaining four members shall be chosen in the following manner:

The members of the bar of this state residing in the judicial circuit of such commission shall elect two of their number to serve as members of said commission, and the governor shall appoint two citizens, not members of the bar, from among the residents of said judicial circuit to serve as members of said commission, the members of the commission shall select one of their number to serve as chairman; and the terms of office of the members of such commission shall be fixed by law, but no law shall increase or diminish the term of any member then in office. No member of any such commission other than a judge shall hold any public office, and no member shall hold any official position in a political party. Every such commission may act only by the concurrence of a majority of its members. The members of such commission shall receive no salary or other compensation for their services but they shall receive their necessary traveling and other expenses incurred while actually engaged in the discharge of their official duties. All such commissions shall be administered, and all elections provided for under this section shall be held and regulated, under such rules as the supreme court shall promulgate. (Adopted August 3, 1976) (This was Sec. 29(d) prior to 1976) Section 25(e). Payment of expenses.—All expenses incurred in administering sections 25(a)–(g), when approved by the supreme court, shall be paid out of the state treasury. The supreme court shall certify such expense to the commissioner of administration, who shall draw his warrant therefor payable out of funds not otherwise appropriated.

Section 25(F). Prohibition of Political Activity by Judges

No judge of any court in this state, appointed to or retained in office in the manner prescribed in sections 25(a)–(g), shall directly or indirectly make any contribution to or hold any office in a political party or organization, or take part in any political campaign.

Section 25(G). Self-Enforceability

All of the provisions of sections 25(a)–(g) shall be self-enforcing except those as to which action by the general assembly may be required.

Section 26. Retirement—Assignment As Senior Judge Or Commissioner

1. All judges other than municipal judges shall retire at the age of seventy years, except as provided in the schedule to this article, under a retirement plan provided by law. 2. All judges may retire at an earlier age authorized by law and may participate in a retirement plan provided by law. 3. Any retired judge, associate circuit judge or commissioner, with his consent, may be assigned by the supreme court as a senior judge to any court in this state or as a special commissioner. When serving as a senior judge he shall have the same powers as an active judge.

SCHEDULE

Section 27. Effective Date and Transition Provisions

Except as otherwise provided in this article, the effective date of this article shall be January 2, 1979.

1. All judges elected in 1978 shall be sworn into office on January 1, 1979.

2. All magistrate courts, probate courts, courts of common pleas, the St. Louis court of criminal correction, and municipal corporation courts shall continue to exist until the effective date of this article at which time said courts shall cease to exist. When such courts cease to exist:

a. The jurisdiction of magistrate courts shall be transferred to the circuit court of the circuit and such courts shall become divisions of the circuit court.
b. The jurisdiction of probate courts within the circuit shall be transferred to the circuit court and such courts shall become divisions of the circuit court.

c. The jurisdiction of St. Louis court of criminal correction and all courts of common pleas shall be transferred to the circuit court for the respective circuit and such courts shall become divisions of the circuit court. The provisions of law relating to practice and procedure of the courts of common pleas shall, until otherwise changed by law, remain in effect and the provision of law relating to practice, procedure, venue, jurisdiction, selection of jurors, election of clerk and provisions for deputies and all other provisions of law relating to the Hannibal Court of Common Pleas shall until otherwise changed by law, remain in effect as to such division of the Marion county circuit court and said division shall be known as division number 2 of the Marion county circuit court instead of the Hannibal Court of Common Pleas.

d. The jurisdiction of municipal courts shall be transferred to the circuit court of the circuit in which such municipality or major geographical area thereof shall be located and, such courts shall become divisions of the circuit court. When such courts cease to exist, all records, papers and files shall be transferred to the circuit court which may designate the place where such records may be maintained.

e. Divisions of the circuit court created by this subsection may be changed hereafter by law.

f. After the effective date of this article, in counties with a population of over thirty thousand and less than sixty-five thousand, the office expenses and salaries of associate circuit judges and their clerks who before the effective date of this article were probate judges shall continue to be paid by the counties.

g. After the effective date of this article, in all counties with a population of over sixty-five thousand and in any city not within a county, the office expenses and salaries of the circuit judges who before the effective date of this article were probate judges in said counties or city, shall be paid by the respective counties or city.

3. Until otherwise provided by law associate circuit judges shall hear all cases or matters, civil and criminal, as now provided by law for magistrates within the county and such additional cases or classes of cases as may be provided by law. Until otherwise provided by law, associate circuit judges shall hear all cases or matters as now provided by law for probate courts within the county, except that in the city of St. Louis, in all first class counties, and all second class counties with a population of over sixty-five thousand, the circuit judge of the probate division of the circuit court shall hear all cases and matters as now provided by law for probate courts within such circuits or counties. An associate circuit judge exercising probate jurisdiction shall, in connection therewith, possess general equitable powers.

Associate circuit judges of the city of St. Louis shall hear all civil and criminal cases as now provided by law for magistrates and the St. Louis court of criminal correction including appeals and preliminary hearings in felony cases and such additional cases or classes of cases as may hereafter be provided by law. Until otherwise provided by law or supreme court rule the practice, procedure, filing fees and administration of causes heard by associate circuit judges within the jurisdiction of former magistrate and probate courts shall be and remain the same as in the court abolished.

4. a. in 1978, all probate judges except those selected under the nonpartisan selection of judges plan shall be elected as provided by law. On the effective date of this article the probate judge of the city of St. Louis and the probate judges of all first class counties and all second class counties with a population of over sixty-five thousand shall become circuit judges of their respective circuits and thereafter shall be selected or elected from the circuit as in the case of other circuit judges and be entitled to the same compensation as provided by law for circuit judges at the time of the effective date of this article until changed by law, and shall have the same powers and jurisdiction as judges of the circuit court. Each judge who served as probate judge and who is in office on the effective date of this article in such city and counties shall continue to serve in the capacity of judge of the probate division of the circuit court until his successor is selected and qualified, provided that with his consent any circuit or associate circuit judge in the circuit at his request may hear, try and dispose of any matter, case or classes of cases assigned to him by such judge of the probate division, and such judge of the probate division with his consent, may hear, try and determine any case within the jurisdiction of the circuit court. On the effective date of this article the probate judges of counties with a population of sixty-five thousand or less shall become associate circuit judges of their respective circuits and thereafter shall be selected or elected from the county as in the case of other associate circuit judges and shall be entitled to the same compensation as that to which they were entitled on the effective date of this article until changed by law.

b. On the effective date of this article, judges of the St. Louis court of criminal correction and judges of the courts of common pleas shall become circuit judges and be entitled to the compensation of circuit judges and shall have the same power and jurisdiction as circuit judges.

c. in 1978, all magistrates shall be elected as provided by law. On the effective date of this article all magistrates who are then in office shall become associate circuit judges and shall serve out the remainder of their terms as such. Each such judge shall be entitled to the same compensation as that to which he was entitled on the effective date of this article until otherwise changed by law.

5. The right to and method of review from a final judgment or appealable order of an associate circuit judge, or municipal judge, when so acting within the jurisdiction of cases heretofore within the jurisdiction of the former magistrate or municipal courts shall, until otherwise provided by law, be de novo before a circuit judge or another associate circuit judge within the circuit except that appeals from an associate circuit judge exercising probate jurisdiction in any circuit, and appeals from any cause from an associate circuit judge as provided by law shall be appealed to the appropriate district of the court of appeals upon a record as authorized by law or supreme court rule. Appeals in misdemeanor cases from the associate circuit judge from the city of St. Louis shall be as now provided until changed by law.

6. The costs of judicial proceedings as provided for in all courts existing before the adoption of this article shall remain in effect with respect to cases which would have been within the jurisdiction of those courts until such costs are otherwise changed by law. Until otherwise provided by law, if a cause could have been filed in more than one court before the effective date of this article, the lower cost structure shall be used in calculating costs; provided, however, that a party instituting a civil suit which would have been within the concurrent jurisdiction of the circuit and magistrate courts prior to the effective date of this article may designate the case as being one to be processed in accordance with procedures and rules appertaining before circuit judges, and the court costs heretofore applicable to such cases in circuit court shall apply.

7. Until the effective date of this article the courts of common pleas, the St. Louis court of criminal corrections, the magistrate courts, the probate courts and the municipal corporation courts shall continue to have the jurisdiction and power provided in the article repealed hereby and provided by the laws and rules enacted thereunder, and shall continue to follow the procedures as provided in such article, laws and rules.

8. Each judge who, on the effective date of this article, becomes a circuit or associate circuit judge in any circuit subject to the provisions of sections 25(a)–(g) of this article shall be eligible for retention in office as a circuit or associate circuit judge respectively by filing in the office of the secretary of state a declaration of candidacy for election not less than sixty days prior to the holding of the general election next preceding the expiration of his term of office. If a majority of those voting on the question vote against retaining him in office, upon the expiration of his term of office, a vacancy shall exist which shall be filled by appointment as provided in section 25(a); otherwise, said judge shall, unless removed for cause, remain in office for the number of years after December thirty-first following such election as is provided for the full term of such office and at the expiration of each such term shall be eligible for retention in office by election in the same manner prescribed by section 25(c)(1). The secretary of state shall certify the name of such judges in accordance with law or in accordance with section 25(c)(2) of this article.

9. On the effective date of this article the judges of the magistrate court and the judges of the probate court in any circuit which selects judges under the nonpartisan selection of judges shall become nonpartisan judges. The judges of the probate courts of the city of St. Louis and all first class counties, and all second class counties with a population of over sixty-five thousand, when such courts cease to exist, and the judges of the St. Louis court of criminal corrections, shall become circuit judges and receive the compensation payable to circuit judges.

9. a. The judges of all municipal corporations courts in office at the time such courts cease to exist and who qualify for office under the provisions of section 21 of this article shall continue in office until the expiration of the terms to which they have been elected or appointed unless otherwise provided by law. When such courts cease to exist, the judges thereof who continue in office shall become municipal judges and shall serve as such until their terms expire or are otherwise removed. They shall receive the compensation now provided until otherwise changed by law. Such compensation shall be paid by the municipality or municipalities they serve. Upon the expiration of their terms, they shall become eligible for retention in office as municipal judges in the same manner as now provided for the selection of municipal judges in the municipality they serve until otherwise provided by law. in the event the municipal judge now serving shall fail, refuse or be disqualified from continuing in office, the municipality may elect or appoint a municipal judge in the same manner as is now provided in that municipality for selection of a municipal judge unless otherwise provided by law. All expenses incidental to the functioning of municipal judges, including the cost of any staff, and their quarters shall be paid and provided by the respective municipalities as now provided for municipal courts until otherwise provided by law. in municipalities with a population of under four hundred thousand which do not have a municipal judge or for which no municipal judge is provided by law, associate circuit judges shall hear and determine violations of municipal ordinances. No associate circuit judge shall, however, act as a municipal judge in any city with a population of four hundred thousand or more until otherwise provided by law.

10. a. 1. Until otherwise provided by law, circuit clerks in each circuit and county shall be selected in the same manner as provided by law on the effective date of this article, except that in counties having a charter form of government, the circuit clerk shall be selected in the manner as provided in the charter of such county.

2. Upon the expiration of the terms of office of the clerk of the circuit court for criminal causes of the city of St. Louis, and the term of the clerk of the St. Louis court of criminal correction, the offices of such clerks shall cease to exist and thereafter the clerk of the circuit court of the city of St. Louis shall have the powers and perform the duties and functions of such clerks and shall serve all divisions of the circuit court, except the courts presided over by an associate circuit judge, the judge of the probate division of the circuit court and by municipal judges.

3. in any division of the circuit court presided over by an associate circuit judge, in the probate division of the circuit court, and in any division presided over by a municipal judge, the clerks and their deputies of the respective divisions shall continue to be selected in the same manner as provided for by law on the effective date of this article until otherwise changed by law.

4. There shall continue to be an office of circuit clerk in each county of the circuit, until otherwise changed by law.

b. Upon the effective date of this article, the office of constable serving magistrate courts is abolished. The functions, powers and duties of such constables shall be transferred to and be performed by the sheriff of the county or the sheriff of the city of St. Louis.

c. Upon the effective date of this article the office of prosecuting attorney of the city of St. Louis shall be abolished and all the duties, powers, and functions of such office shall be transferred to the circuit attorney of the city of St. Louis who shall have such powers and perform such functions and duties as the prosecuting attorney of the city of St. Louis.

d. No election shall be held in 1978 for the offices which are abolished by this subsection 10.

11. The commissioners of the supreme court holding office on the effective date of this article shall continue to hold office as commissioners of the court until the end of their terms, and shall be eligible for reappointment thereafter from term to term under existing law until retirement, death, resignation or removal for cause. Upon the occurrence of such vacancy in the office of commissioner of the supreme court, such office shall cease to exist. Commissioners, in addition to their regular duties, shall be subject to temporary assignment for the performance of judicial duties as special judges of the supreme court, court of appeals, or circuit court on order of the supreme court. During such temporary assignments, commissioners sitting as special judges shall have the same powers, duties, and responsibilities as are vested by law in the regular judges of the courts to which they are assigned.

12. The boundaries and territorial jurisdiction of the districts of the court of appeals and of the judicial circuits as they exist on the effective date of this article shall be continued in effect until such time as changed by law.

13. The commission on retirement, removal and discipline and the nonpartisan appellate and circuit judicial commissions in existence on the effective date of this article shall continue to exist, and the terms of office for such commissions shall continue in effect.

14. "Judge" as used in sections 20, 24 and 26 of this article shall include commissioners of the supreme court.

15. Nothing in this article shall deprive any person of any right or privilege to retire and the retirement benefits to which he was entitled immediately prior to the effective date of this article.

16. A municipal corporation with a population of under four hundred thousand shall have the right to enforce its ordinances and to conduct prosecutions before an associate circuit judge in the absence of a municipal judge and in appellate courts under the process authorized or provided by this article and shall receive and retain any fines to which it may be entitled. All court costs shall be paid to and deposited monthly in the state treasury. No filing fees shall be charged in such prosecutions unless and until provided for by a law enacted after the adoption of this article.

17. Until otherwise provided by law, the circuit courts shall continue to have jurisdiction to review administrative decisions, findings, rules, and orders in the manner and practice and pursuant to the laws and rules then in force at the time this article becomes effective.

18. All rights, claims, causes of action and obligations existing and all contracts, prosecutions, recognizances and other instruments executed or entered into and all indictments, informations, and complaints which shall have been filed and all actions which shall have been instituted and all fines, penalties and forfeitures assessed, due or owing prior to the effective date of this article shall continue to be as valid as if this article had not been adopted.

19. The general assembly may enact such laws and make such appropriations as may be necessary to carry out the provisions of this article.

20. All laws and rules inconsistent with the provisions of this article shall, on the effective date hereof, be and are repealed. Except to the extent inconsistent with the provisions of this article, all provisions of law and rules of court in force on the effective date of this amendment shall continue in effect until superseded in a manner authorized by the constitution or by law.

21. in the event that a new district of the court of appeals is established, the judges presently serving on any district of the court of appeals shall continue to be judges of the court of appeals to which appointed although they are not residents of the court of appeals district in which they serve.

22. Until otherwise provided by law, in any cause heard and determined by an associate circuit judge, the associate circuit judge shall utilize electronic, magnetic, or mechanical sound or video recording devices for the purpose of preserving the record. Electronic, magnetic, or mechanical recording devices shall be approved by the office of state courts administrator prior to their utilization by any associate circuit judge.

23. Each circuit in which judges are selected under the nonpartisan court plan, on the effective date of this article, including the circuits of Platte county, Clay county, and St. Louis county, shall continue under the nonpartisan court plan until and unless such method of selection of judges is discontinued by the voters of the circuit as provided by sections 25(a)–(g) of this article.

24. Judges, other than municipal judges, not selected under the provisions of sections 25(a)–(g) of this article who on the effective day of this article or within six months thereafter, are seventy years of age or older, may petition the commission on retirement, removal and discipline to continue to serve until age seventy-six if he has not completed a total of twelve years of service as a judge. Judges, other than municipal judges, not selected under the provisions of sections 25(a)–(g) of this article who are in office on the effective date of this article, may, within six months before attaining the age of seventy years, petition the commission on retirement, removal, and discipline to be allowed to serve after he has attained that age until age seventy-six or has completed a total of twelve years of service as a judge, whichever shall first occur. If the commission finds the petitioner to be able to perform his duties and approves such service, the petitioner may continue to serve as such a judge until age seventy-six if he has not completed a total of twelve years of service as a judge at such age. No such judge shall be permitted to serve as such a judge beyond the age of seventy-six years regardless of whether or not he has completed a total of twelve years except for the purpose of completing the term to which he was elected or appointed.

ARTICLE VI: LOCAL GOVERNMENT

Section 1. Recognition of Existing Counties

The existing counties are hereby recognized as legal subdivisions of the state.

Section 2. Continuation of Existing Organization of Counties

The existing organization of counties shall continue until further provisions applicable thereto shall be provided, as authorized in this constitution.

Section 3. Consolidation of Counties—Allocation of Liabilities

Two or more counties may be consolidated by vote of a majority of the qualified electors voting thereon in each county affected, but no such vote shall be taken more than once in five years. The former areas shall be held responsible for their respective outstanding liabilities as provided by law.

Section 4. Division Or Diminution of Counties

No county shall be divided or have any portion stricken therefrom except by vote of a majority of the qualified electors voting thereon in each county affected.

Section 5. Dissolution of Counties—Annexation

A county may be dissolved by vote of two-thirds of the qualified electors of the county voting thereon, and when so dissolved all or portions thereof may be annexed to the adjoining county or counties as provided by law.

Section 6. Removal of County Seats

No county seat shall be removed except by vote of two-thirds of the qualified electors of the county voting thereon at a general election, but no such vote shall be taken more than once in five years.

Section 7. County Courts—Number of Members—Powers and Du Ties

in each county not framing and adopting its own charter or adopting an alternative form of county government, there shall be elected a county court of three members which shall manage all county business as prescribed by law, and keep an accurate record of its proceedings. The voters of any county may reduce the number of members to one or two as provided by law.

Section 8. Classification of Counties—Revisions to Article Vi Passed by The 88th General Assembly to be Retroactive

Provision shall be made by general laws for the organization and classification of counties except as provided in section 18(a) or section 18(m) of this article or otherwise in this constitution. The number of classes shall not exceed four, and the organization and powers of each class shall be defined by general laws so that all counties within the same class shall possess the same powers and be subject to the same restrictions. The revisions to this article submitted by the first regular session of the eighty-eighth general assembly are intended to be applied retro actively and no law adopted by the general assembly or ordinance or order adopted by the governing body of a county shall be declared unconstitutional if such law, ordinance or order would have been constitutional had this section, as amended, been in effect at the time the law was passed, unless the law is declared unconstitutional pursuant to a different provision of this constitution.

Section 9. Alternative Forms of County Government

Alternative forms of county government for the counties of any particular class and the method of adoption thereof may be provided by law.

Section 10. Terms of City and County Offices

The terms of city or county offices shall not exceed four years.

Section 11. Compensation of County Officers—Increases in Compensation Not to Require Additional Services—Statement of Fees and Salaries

1. Except in counties which frame, adopt and amend a charter for their own government, the compensation of all county officers shall either be prescribed by law or be established by each county pursuant to law adopted by the general assembly. A law which would authorize an increase in the compensation of county officers shall not be construed as requiring a new activity or service or an increase in the level of any activity or service within the meaning of this constitution. Every such officer shall file a sworn statement in detail, of fees collected and salaries paid to his necessary deputies or assistants, as provided by law.

2. Upon approval of this amendment by the voters of Missouri the compensation of county officials, or their duly appointed successor, elected at the general election in 1984 or 1986 may be increased during that term in accordance with any law adopted by the general assembly or, in counties which have adopted a charter for their own government, in accordance with such charter, notwithstanding the provisions of section 13 of article VII of the Constitution of Missouri.

Section 12. Officers Compensated Only by Salaries in Certain Counties

All public officers in the city of St. Louis and all state and county officers in counties having 100,000 or more inhabitants, excepting public administrators and notaries public, shall be compensated for their services by salaries only. Section 13. Compensation of officers in criminal matters—fees.—All state and county officers, except constables and justices of the peace, charged with the investigation, arrest, prosecution, custody, care, feeding, commitment, or transportation of persons accused of or convicted of a criminal offense shall be compensated for their official services only by salaries, and any fees and charges collected by any such officers in such cases shall be paid into the general revenue fund entitled to receive the same, as provided by law. Any fees earned by any such officers in civil matters may be retained by them as provided by law.

Section 14. Joint Participation by Counties in Common Enterprises

by vote of a majority of the qualified electors voting thereon in each county affected, any contiguous counties, not exceeding ten, may join in performing any common function or service, including the purchase, construction and maintenance of hospitals, alms houses, road machinery and any other county property, and by separate vote may join in the common employment of any county officer or employee common to each of the counties. The county courts shall administer the delegated powers and allocate the costs among the counties. Any county may withdraw from such joint participation by vote of a majority of its qualified electors voting thereon.

Section 15. Classification of Cities and Towns—Uniform Laws—Change From Special to General Law

The general assembly shall provide by general laws for the organization and classification of cities and towns. The number of such classes shall not exceed four; and the powers of each class shall be defined by general laws so that all such municipal corporations of the same class shall possess the same powers and be subject to the same restrictions. The general assembly shall also make provisions, by general law, whereby any city, town or village, existing by virtue of any special or local law, may elect to become subject to, and be governed by, the general laws relating to such corporations.

Section 16. Cooperation by Local Governments With Other Governmental Units

Any municipality or political subdivision of this state may contract and cooperate with other municipalities or political subdivisions thereof, or with other states or their municipalities or political subdivisions, or with the United States, for the planning, development, construction, acquisition or operation of any public improvement or facility, or for a common service, in the manner provided by law.

Section 17. Consolidation and Separation As Between Municipalities and Other Political Subdivisions

The government of any city, town or village not in a county framing, adopting and amending a charter for its own government, may be consolidated or separated, in whole or in part, with or from that of the county or other political subdivision in which such city, town or village is situated, as provided by law.

SPECIAL CHARTERS

Section 18(A). County Government by Special Charter—Limitations—Counties Adopting Charter Or Constitutional Form Shall be A Separate Class of Counties From Classification System

Any county having more than 85,000 inhabitants, according to the census of the United States, may frame and adopt and amend a charter for its own government as provided in this article, and upon such adoption shall be a body corporate and politic. in addition and as an alternative to the foregoing, any county which attains first class county status and maintains such status for at least two years shall be authorized to frame and adopt and amend a charter for its own government as provided by this article, and upon such adoption by a vote of the qualified electors of such county shall be a body corporate and politic. Counties which adopt or which have adopted a charter or constitutional form of government shall be a separate class of counties outside of the classification system established under section 8 of this article.

Section 18(B). Provisions Required in County Charters—Exception

The charter shall provide for its amendment, for the form of the county government, the number, kinds, manner of selection, terms of office and salaries of the county officers, and for the exercise of all powers and duties of counties and county officers prescribed by the constitution and laws of the state; however, such charter shall, except for the charter of any county with a charter form of government and with more than six hundred thousand but fewer than seven hundred thousand inhabitants, require the assessor of the county to be an elected officer.

Section 18(C). Provisions Authorized in County Charters—Participation by County in Government of Other Local Units

The charter may provide for the vesting and exercise of legislative power pertaining to any and all services and functions of any municipality or political subdivision, except school districts, in the part of the county outside incorporated cities; and it may provide, or authorize its governing body to provide, the terms upon which the county may contract with any municipality or political subdivision in the county and perform any of the services and functions of any such municipality or political subdivision. The charter may provide for the vesting and exercise of legislative power pertaining to any and all services and functions of any municipality or political subdivision, except school districts, throughout the entire county within as well as outside incorporated municipalities; any such charter provision shall set forth the limits within which the municipalities may exercise the same power collaterally and coextensively. When such a proposition is submitted to the voters of the county the ballot shall contain a clear definition of the power, function or service to be performed and the method by which it will be financed.

Section 18(D). Taxation Under County Charters

The county shall only impose such taxes as it is authorized to impose by the constitution or by law.

Section 18(E). Laws Affecting Charter Counties—Limitations

Laws shall be enacted providing for free and open elections in such counties, and laws may be enacted providing the number and salaries of the judicial officers therein as provided by this constitution and by law, but no law shall provide for any other office or employee of the county or fix the salary of any of its officers or employees.

Section 18(F). Petitions for Charter Commissions—Signatures Required—Procedure

Whenever a petition for a commission, signed by qualified electors of the county numbering ten percent of the total vote for governor in the county at the last preceding general election, is filed with the county commission or other governing body, the officer or body canvassing election returns shall forthwith finally determine the sufficiency thereof and certify the result to the governing body, which shall give immediate written notice of the petition to the circuit judges of the county.

Section 18(G). Charter Commission—Appointment, Number and Qualification of Members

Within sixty days thereafter said judges shall appoint a commission to frame the charter, consisting of fourteen qualified electors who shall serve without pay and be equally divided between the two political parties casting the greater number of votes for governor at the last preceding general election.

Section 18(H). Adoption of Charter—Special Election—Manner of Submission

The charter framed by the commission shall take effect on the day fixed therein and shall supersede any existing charter or government, if approved by vote of a majority of the qualified electors of the county voting thereon at a special election held on a day fixed by the commission and not less than thirty days after the completion of the charter nor more than one year from the day of the selection of the commission. The commission may submit for separate vote any parts of the charter, or any alternative sections or articles, and the alternative sections or articles receiving the larger affirmative vote shall prevail if a charter is adopted.

Section 18(I). Notice of Special Charter Election

The body canvassing election returns shall publish notice of the election at least once a week for at least three weeks in at least two newspapers of general circulation in the county, the last publication to be not more than three nor less than two weeks next preceding the election.

Section 18(j). Certificates of adoption of charter— recordation and deposit— judicial notice

Duplicate certificates shall be made, setting forth the charter adopted and its ratification, signed by the officer or members of the body canvassing election returns; one of such certified copies shall be deposited in the office of the secretary of state and the other, after being recorded in the records of the county, shall be deposited among the archives of the county and all courts shall take judicial notice thereof. This section shall also apply to any amendment to the charter.

Section 18(K). Amendments of County Charters

All amendments to such charter approved by the voters shall become a part of the charter at the time and under the conditions fixed in the amendment.

Section 18(L). Limitation On Resubmission After Defeat of Charter

No charter shall be submitted to the electors within the two years next following the election at which a charter was defeated.

Section 18(M). County of The First Classification May Provide A County Constitution—Content, Procedure, Limitations

Any county of the first classification may adopt an alternative form of government to that provided in sections 18(a)–(g) of this article and frame a county constitution as provided in sections 18(m)–(r) of this article. The constitution may provide for the vesting of any and all powers the general assembly has the authority to confer, provided such powers are not limited or denied by laws of this state, except those powers to regulate and provide for free and open elections. A county approving the alternative form of government and adopting a county constitution in the manner prescribed by sections 18(m)–(r) of this article shall only impose such taxes as it is authorized by the constitution and law to impose. The county commission of such a county may authorize the submission of the question by placing it on the ballot on any election day established by law. The circuit judges of the circuit where such county is located shall establish a county constitution commission if the qualified voters of the county approve the question.

Section 18(N). Circuit Judges May Appoint Constitution Commission, Members, Qualifications

If the question is approved, the circuit judges of the circuit where such county is located shall, within sixty days after certification of the election results by the election authority, appoint a commission to frame the county constitution, consisting of fourteen residents of the county who shall serve without pay and be equally divided between the two political parties casting the greater number of votes for governor at the last preceding gubernatorial election.

Section 18(O). County Constitution, Effective When—Submission to Electorate for Separate Vote On Any Part Or Alternative Sections

The county constitution framed by the commission shall take effect on the day fixed therein and shall supersede any existing charter, county constitution or government, if approved by the majority of the qualified voters of the county voting thereon. The county constitution shall be submitted by the county constitution commission to the election authority of the county not later than thirty days after the completion of the county constitution and not more than one year from the date of the selection of the county constitution commission by the circuit court. The commission may submit for separate vote any part of the county constitution, or any alternative sections or articles, and the alternative sections or articles receiving the larger affirmative vote shall prevail if a constitution is adopted.

Section 18(P). Publication Requirements for Text of Constitution—Election to Adopt Procedure

in addition to notices required under the election laws of the state, the election authority shall publish the full text of the county constitution in each newspaper of general circulation in the county at least once a week for at least three weeks, the last publication to be not more than three nor less than two weeks immediately preceding the election. Except as otherwise provided herein, the election shall be conducted under Missouri election law.

Section 18(Q). Constitution May be Adopted Or Rejected by Voters—Resubmission Procedure

If a majority of the votes cast by the qualified voters voting on the county constitution are in favor of the proposal, then the county constitution shall be adopted. If a majority of the votes cast by the qualified voters voting thereon are opposed to the proposal, the county constitution shall not be adopted. A proposal to create a county constitution may not be resubmitted to the voters except after the voters approve the selection of a commission to draft a county constitution as provided in section 18(m) of this article and such proposal shall not be resubmitted to the voters until two years after the proposed county constitution has been rejected.

Section 18(R). Certified Copies of County Constitution to be Filed, Where—Amendments to Constitution, Procedure

Duplicate certificates shall be made, setting forth the adopted county constitution, and its ratification signed by the election authority of the county after canvassing election returns. One of the certified copies shall be deposited in the office of the secretary of state and the other, after being recorded in the records of the county, shall be deposited among the archives of the county and all courts shall take judicial notice thereof. Amendments shall be certified and deposited in the same way. Amendments to the county constitution shall be approved by the voters and shall become part of the county constitution at the time and under the conditions fixed in each amendment.

LOCAL GOVERNMENT

Section 19. Certain Cities May Adopt Charter Form of Government—Procedure to Frame and Adopt—Notice Required—Effect of

Any city having more than five thousand inhabitants or any other incorporated city as may be provided by law may frame and adopt a charter for its own government. The legislative body of the city may, by ordinance, submit to the voters the question: "Shall a commission be chosen to frame a charter?" If the ordinance takes effect more than sixty days before the next election, the question shall be submitted at such election and if not, then at the next general election thereafter, except as herein otherwise provided. The question shall also be submitted on a petition signed by ten percent of the qualified electors of the city, filed with the body or official in charge of the city elections. If the petition prays for a special election and is signed by twenty percent of the qualified electors, a special election shall be held not less than sixty nor more than ninety days after the filing of the petition. The number of electors required to sign any petition shall be based upon the total number of electors voting at the last preceding general city election. The election body or official shall forthwith finally determine the sufficiency of the petition. The question, and the names or the groups of names of the electors of the city who are candidates for the commission, shall be printed on the same ballot without party designation. Candidates for the commission shall be nominated by petition signed by not less than two percent of the qualified electors voting at the next preceding city election, and filed with the election body or official at least thirty days prior to the election; provided that the signatures of one thousand electors shall be sufficient to nominate a candidate. If a majority of the electors voting on the question vote in the affirmative, the thirteen candidates receiving the highest number of votes shall constitute the commission. On the death, resignation or inability of any member to serve, the remaining members of the commission shall select the successor. All necessary expenses of the commission shall be paid by the city. The charter so framed shall be submitted to the electors of the city at an election held at the time fixed by the commission, but not less than thirty days subsequent to the completion of the charter nor more than one year from the date of the election of the commission. The commission may submit for separate vote any parts of the charter, or any alternative sections or articles, and the alternative sections or articles receiving the larger affirmative vote shall prevail if a charter is adopted. If the charter be approved by the voters it shall become the charter of such city at the time fixed therein and shall supersede any existing charter and amendments thereof. Duplicate certificates shall be made, setting forth the charter adopted and its ratification, signed by the chief magistrate of the city, and authenticated by its corporate seal. One of such certified copies shall be deposited in the office of the secretary of state and the other, after being recorded in the records of the city, shall be deposited among the archives of the city and all courts shall take judicial notice thereof. The notice of the election shall be published at least once a week on the same day of the week for at least three weeks in some daily or weekly newspaper of general circulation in the city or county, admitted to the post office as second class matter, regularly and consecutively published for at least three years, and having a list of bona fide subscribers who have voluntarily paid or agreed to pay a stated price for a subscription for a definite period of time, the last publication to be within two weeks of the election.

Section 19(A). Power of Charter Cities, How Limited

Any city which adopts or has adopted a charter for its own government, shall have all powers which the general assembly of the state of Missouri has authority to confer upon any city, provided such powers are consistent with the constitution of this state and are not limited or denied either by the charter so adopted or by statute. Such a city shall, in addition to its home rule powers, have all powers conferred by law.

Section 20. Amendment to City Charters—Procedure to Submit and Adopt

Amendments of any city charter adopted under the foregoing provisions may be submitted to the electors by a commission as provided for a complete charter. Amendments may also be proposed by the legislative body of the city or by petition of not less than ten percent of the registered qualified electors of the city, filed with the body or official having charge of the city elections, setting forth the proposed amendment. The legislative body shall at once provide, by ordinance, that any amendment so proposed shall be submitted to the electors at the next election held in the city not less than sixty days after its passage, or at a special election held as provided for a charter. Any amendment approved by a majority of the qualified electors voting thereon, shall become a part of the charter at the time and under the conditions fixed in the amendment; and sections or articles may be submitted separately or in the alternative and determined as provided for a complete charter.

Section 21. Reclamation of Blighted, Substandard Or Insanitary Areas

Laws may be enacted, and any city or county operating under a constitutional charter may enact ordinances, providing for the clearance, replanning, reconstruction, redevelopment and rehabilitation of blighted, substandard or insanitary areas, and for recreational and other facilities incidental or appurtenant thereto, and for taking or permitting the taking, by eminent domain, of property for such purposes, and when so taken the fee simple title to the property shall vest in the owner, who may sell or otherwise dispose of the property subject to such restrictions as may be deemed in the public interest.

Section 22. Laws Affecting Charter Cities—Officers and Employees

No law shall be enacted creating or fixing the powers, duties or compensation of any municipal office or employment, for any city framing or adopting its own charter under this or any previous constitution, and all such offices or employments heretofore created shall cease at the end of the terms of any present incumbents.

FINANCES

Section 23. Limitation On Ownership of Corporate Stock, Use of Credit and Grants of Public Funds by Local Governments

No county, city or other political corporation or subdivision of the state shall own or subscribe for stock in any corporation or association, or lend its credit or grant public money or thing of value to or in aid of any corporation, association or individual, except as provided in this constitution.

Section 23(A). Cities May Acquire and Furnish Industrial Plants—Indebtedness for

by vote of two-thirds of the qualified electors thereof voting thereon, any county, city or incorporated town or village in this state may become indebted for and may purchase, construct, extend or improve plants to be leased or otherwise disposed of pursuant to law to private persons or corporations for manufacturing, warehousing and industrial development purposes, including the real estate, buildings, fixtures and machinery; and the indebtedness incurred hereunder shall not be subject to the provisions of sections 26(a), 26(b), 26(c), 26(d) and 26(e) of Article VI of this Constitution; but any indebtedness incurred hereunder for this purpose shall not exceed ten percent of the value of taxable tangible property in the county, city, or incorporated town or village as shown by the last completed assessment for state and county purposes.

Section 24. Annual Budgets and Reports of Local Government and Municipally Owned Utilities—Audits

As prescribed by law all counties, cities, other legal subdivisions of the state, and public utilities owned and operated by such subdivisions shall have an annual budget, file annual reports of their financial transactions, and be audited.

Section 25. Limitation On Use of Credit and Grant of Public Funds by Local Governments—Pensions and Retirement Plans for Employees of Certain Cities and Counties

No county, city or other political corporation or subdivision of the state shall be authorized to lend its credit or grant public money or property to any private individual, association or corporation except as provided in Article VI, Section 23(a) and except that the general assembly may authorize any county, city or other political corporation or subdivision to provide for the retirement or pensioning of its officers and employees and the surviving spouses and children of deceased officers and employees and may also authorize payments from any public funds into a fund or funds for paying benefits upon retirement, disability or death to persons employed and paid out of any public fund for educational services and to their beneficiaries or estates; and except, also, that any county of the first class is authorized to provide for the creation and establishment of death benefits, pension and retirement plans for all its salaried employees, and the surviving spouses and minor children of such deceased employees; and except also, any county, city or political corporation or subdivision may provide for the payment of periodic cost of living increases in pension and retirement benefits paid under this section to its retired officers and employees and spouses of deceased officers and employees, provided such pension and retirement systems will remain actuarially sound.

Section 26(A). Limitation On Indebtedness of Local Governments Without Popular Vote

No county, city, incorporated town or village, school district or other political corporation or subdivision of the state shall become indebted in an amount exceeding in any year the income and revenue provided for such year plus any unencumbered balances from previous years, except as otherwise provided in this constitution.

Section 26(B). Limitation On Indebtedness of Local Government Authorized by Popular Vote

Any county, city, incorporated town or village or other political corporation or subdivision of the state, by vote of the qualified electors thereof voting thereon, may become indebted in an amount not to exceed five percent of the value of taxable tangible property therein as shown by the last completed assessment for state or county purposes, except that a school district by a vote of the qualified electors voting thereon may become indebted in an amount not to exceed fifteen percent of the value of such taxable tangible property. for elections referred to in this section the vote required shall be four-sevenths at the general municipal election day, primary or general elections and two-thirds at all other elections.

Section 26(C). Additional Indebtedness of Counties and Cities When Authorized by Popular Vote

Any county or city, by a vote of the qualified electors thereof voting thereon, may incur an additional indebtedness for county or city purposes not to exceed five percent of the taxable tangible property shown as provided in section 26(b). for elections referred to in this section the vote required shall be four-sevenths at the general municipal election day, primary or general elections and two-thirds at all other elections.

Section 26(D). Additional Indebtedness of Cities for Public Improvements— Benefit Districts—Special Assessments

Any city, by vote of the qualified electors thereof voting thereon, may become indebted not exceeding in the aggregate an additional ten percent of the value of the taxable tangible property shown as provided in section 26(b), for the purpose of acquiring rights-of-way, constructing, extending and improving the streets and avenues and acquiring rights-of-way, constructing, extending and improving sanitary or storm sewer systems. The governing body of the city may provide that any portion or all of the cost of any such improvement be levied and assessed by the governing body on property benefited by such improvement, and the city shall collect any special assessments so levied and shall use the same to reimburse the city for the amount paid or to be paid by it on the bonds of the city issued for such improvement. for elections referred to in this section the vote required shall be four-sevenths at the general municipal election day, primary or general elections and two-thirds at all other elections.

Section 26(E). Additional Indebtedness of Cities for Municipally Owned Water and Light Plants—Limitations

Any city, by vote of the qualified electors thereof voting thereon, may incur an indebtedness in an amount not to exceed an additional ten percent of the value of the taxable tangible property shown as provided in section 26(b), for the purpose of paying all or any part of the cost of purchasing or constructing waterworks, electric or other light plants to be owned exclusively by the city, provided the total general obligation indebtedness of the city shall not exceed twenty percent of the assessed valuation. for elections referred to in this section the vote required shall be four-sevenths at the general municipal election day, primary or general elections and two-thirds at all other elections.

Section 26(F). Annual Tax to Pay and Retire Obligations Within Twenty Years

Before incurring any indebtedness every county, city, incorporated town or village, school district, or other political corporation or subdivision of the state shall provide for the collection of an annual tax on all taxable tangible property therein sufficient to pay the interest and principal of the indebtedness as they fall due, and to retire the same within twenty years from the date contracted.

Section 26(G). Contest of Elections to Authorize Indebtedness

All elections under this article may be contested as provided by law.

LOCAL GOVERNMENT

Section 27. Political Subdivision Revenue Bonds for Utility, Industrial and Airport Purposes—Restrictions

Any city or incorporated town or village in this state, by vote of a majority of the qualified electors thereof voting thereon, and any joint board or commission, established by a joint contract between municipalities or political subdivisions in this state, by compliance with then applicable requirements of law, may issue and sell its negotiable interest bearing revenue bonds for the purpose of paying all or part of the cost of purchasing, construction, extending or improving any of the following projects:

(1) Revenue producing water, sewer, gas or electric light works, heating or power plants;

(2) Plants to be leased or otherwise disposed of pursuant to law to private persons or corporations for manufacturing and industrial development purposes, including the real estate, buildings, fixtures and machinery; or

(3) Airports. The project shall be owned by the municipality or by the cooperating municipalities or political subdivisions or the joint board or commission, either exclusively or jointly or by participation with cooperatives or municipally owned or public utilities, the cost of operation and maintenance and the principal and interest of the bonds to be payable solely from the revenues derived by the municipality or by the cooperating municipalities or political subdivisions or the joint board or commission from the operation of the utility or the lease or operation of the project. The bonds shall not constitute an indebtedness of the state, or of any political subdivision thereof, and neither the full faith and credit nor the taxing power of the state or of any political subdivision thereof is pledged to the payment of or the interest on such bonds. Nothing in this section shall affect the ability of the public service commission to regulate investor-owned utilities.

Section 27(A). Political Subdivision Revenue Bonds Issued for Utilities and Airports, Restrictions

Any county, city or incorporated town or village in this state, by vote of a majority of the qualified electors thereof voting thereon, may issue and sell its negotiable interest bearing revenue bonds for the purpose of paying all or part of the cost of purchasing, constructing, extending or improving any of the following:

(1) revenue producing water, gas or electric light works, heating or power plants; or

(2) airports; to be owned exclusively by the county, city or incorporated town or village, the cost of operation and maintenance and the principal and interest of the bonds to be payable solely from the revenues derived by the county, city or incorporated town or village from the operation of the utility or airport.

Section 27(B). Political Subdivision Revenue Bonds Issued for Industrial Development, Restriction

Any county, city or incorporated town or village in this state, by a majority vote of the governing body thereof, may issue and sell its negotiable interest bearing revenue bonds for the purpose of paying all or part of the cost of purchasing, constructing, extending or improving any facility to be leased or otherwise disposed of pursuant to law to private persons or corporations for manufacturing, commercial, warehousing and industrial development purposes, including the real estate, buildings, fixtures and machinery. The cost of operation and maintenance and the principal and interest of the bonds shall be payable solely from the revenues derived by the county, city, or incorporated town or village from the lease or other disposal of the facility.

Section 27(C). Revenue Bonds Defined

As used in article VI, sections 27(a) and 27(b), the term "revenue bonds" means bonds neither the interest nor the principal of which is an indebtedness or obligation of the issuing county, city or incorporated town or village.

Section 28. Refunding Bonds

for the purpose of refunding, extending, and unifying the whole or any part of its valid bonded indebtedness any county, city, school district, or other political corporation or subdivision of the state, under terms and conditions prescribed by law may issue refunding bonds not exceeding in amount the principal of the outstanding indebtedness to be refunded and the accrued interest to the date of such refunding bonds. The governing authority shall provide for the payment of interest at not to exceed the same rate, and the principal of such refunding bonds, in the same manner as was provided for the payment of interest and principal of the bonds refunded.

Section 29. Application of Funds Derived From Public Debts

The moneys arising from any loan, debt, or liability contracted by the state, or any county, city, or other political subdivision, shall be applied to the purposes for which they were obtained, or to the repayment of such debt or liability, and not otherwise.

CITY AND COUNTY OF ST. LOUIS

Section 30(A). Powers Conferred With Respect to Intergovernmental Relations—Procedure for Selection of Board of Freeholders

The people of the city of St. Louis and the people of the county of St. Louis shall have power:

(1) to consolidate the territories and governments of the city and county into one political subdivision under the municipal government of the city of St. Louis; or,

(2) to extend the territorial boundaries of the county so as to embrace the territory within the city and to reorganize and consolidate the county governments of the city and county, and adjust their relations as thus united, and thereafter the city may extend its limits in the manner provided by law for other cities; or,

(3) to enlarge the present or future limits of the city by annexing thereto part of the territory of the county, and to confer upon the city exclusive jurisdiction of the territory so annexed to the city; or,

(4) to establish a metropolitan district or districts for the functional administration of services common to the area included therein; or,

(5) to formulate and adopt any other plan for the partial or complete government of all or any part of the city and the county. The power so given shall be exercised by the vote of the people of the city and county upon a plan prepared by a board of freeholders consisting of nineteen members, nine of whom shall be electors of the city and nine electors of the county and one an elector of some other county. Upon the filing with the officials in general charge of elections in the city of a petition proposing the exercise of the powers hereby granted, signed by registered voters of the city in such number as shall equal three percent of the total vote cast in the city at the last general election for governor, and the certification thereof by the election officials to the mayor, and to the governor, then, within ten days after the certification the mayor shall, with the approval of a majority of the board of aldermen, appoint the city's nine members of the board, not more than five of whom shall be members of or affiliated with the same political party. Each member so appointed shall be given a certificate certifying his appointment signed by the mayor and attested by the seal of the city. Upon the filing with the officials in general charge of elections in the county of a similar petition signed by registered voters of the county, in such number as shall equal three percent of the total vote cast in the county at the last general election for governor, and the certification thereof by the county election officials to the county supervisor of the county and to the governor, within ten days after the certification, the county supervisor shall, with the approval of a majority of the county council, appoint the county's nine members of the board, not more than five of whom shall be members of or affiliated with the same political party. Each member so appointed shall be given a certificate of his appointment signed by the county supervisor and attested by the seal of the county.

Section 30(B). Appointment of Member by Governor—Meetings of Board—Vacancies—Compensation and Reimbursement of Members—Preparation of Plan—Taxation of Real Estate Affected—Submission At Special Elections—Effect of Adoption—Certification and Recordation—Judicial Notice

Upon certification of the filing of such similar petitions by the officials in general charge of elections of the city and the county, the governor shall appoint one member of the board who shall be a resident of the state, but shall not reside in either the city or the county, who shall be given a certificate of his appointment signed by the governor and attested by the seal of the state. The freeholders of the city and county shall fix reasonable compensation and expenses for the freeholder appointed by the governor and the cost shall be paid equally by the city and county. The appointment of the board shall be completed within thirty days after the certification of the filing of the petition, and at ten o'clock on the second Monday after their appointment the members of the board shall meet in the chamber of the board of aldermen in the city hall of the city and shall proceed with the discharge of their duties, and shall meet at such other times and places as shall be agreed upon. On the death, resignation or inability of any member of the board to serve, the ap pointing authority shall select the successor. The board shall prepare and propose a plan for the execution of the powers herein granted and for the adjustment of all matters and issues arising thereunder. The members of the board shall receive no compensation for their services as members, but the necessary expenses of the board shall be paid one-half by the county and one-half by the city on vouchers signed by the chairman of the board. The plan shall be signed in duplicate by the board or a majority thereof, and one copy shall be returned to the officials having general charge of elections in the city, and the other to such officials in the county, within one year after the appointment of the board. Said election officials shall cause separate elections to be held in the city and county, on the day fixed by the freeholders, at which the plan shall be submitted to the qualified voters of the city and county separately. The elections shall not be less than ninety days after the filing of the plan with said officials, and not on or within seventy days of any state or county primary or general election day in the city or county. The plan shall provide for the assessment and taxation of real estate in accordance with the use to which it is being put at the time of the assessment, whether agricultural, industrial or other use, giving due regard to the other provisions of this constitution. If a majority of the qualified electors of the city voting thereon, and a majority of the qualified electors of the county voting thereon at the separate elections shall vote for the plan, then, at such time as shall be prescribed therein, the same shall become the organic law of the territory therein defined, and shall take the place of and supersede all laws, charter provisions and ordinances inconsistent therewith relating to said territory. If the plan be adopted, copies thereof, certified to by said election officials of the city and county, shall be de posited in the office of the secretary of state and recorded in the office of the recorder of deeds for the city, and in the office of the recorder of deeds of the present county, and the courts of this state shall take judicial notice thereof.

CITY OF ST. LOUIS

Section 31. Recognition of City of St. Louis As Now Existing Both As A City and As A County

The city of St. Louis, as now existing, is recognized both as a city and as a county unless otherwise changed in accordance with the provisions of this constitution. As a city it shall continue for city purposes with its present charter, subject to changes and amendments provided by the constitution or by law, and with the powers, organization, rights and privileges permitted by this constitution or by law. As a county, it shall not be required to adopt a county charter but may, except for the office of circuit attorney, amend or revise its present charter to provide for the number, kinds, manner of selection, terms of office and salaries of its county officers, and for the exercise of all powers and duties of counties and county officers prescribed by the constitution and laws of the state.

Section 32(A). Amendment of Charter of St. Louis

The charter of the city of St. Louis now existing, or as hereafter amended or revised, may be amended or revised for city or county purposes from time to time by proposals therefor submitted by the lawmaking body of the city to the qualified voters thereof, at a general or special election held at least sixty days after the publication of such proposals, and accepted by three-fifths of the qualified electors voting for or against each of said amendments or revisions so submitted.

Section 32(B). Revision of Charter of St. Louis—Officers to Complete Terms and Staff Given Opportunity for City Employment

in the event of any amendment or revision of the charter of the city of St. Louis which shall reorganize any county office and/or transfer any or all of the duties, powers and functions of any county officer who is then in office, the officer shall serve out the remainder of his or her term, and the amendment or revision of the charter of the city of St. Louis shall take effect, as to such office, upon the expiration of the term of such office holder. in the event of any amendment or revision of the charter of the city of St. Louis which shall reorganize any county office and/or transfer any or all of the duties, powers and functions of any county officer, all of the staff of such office shall be afforded the opportunity to become employees of the city of St. Louis with their individual seniority and compensation unaffected and on such other comparable terms and conditions as may be fair and equitable.

Section 32(C). Effect of Revision On Retirement

An amendment or revision adopted pursuant to section 32(a) of this article shall not deprive any person of any right or privilege to retire and to retirement benefits, if any, to which he or she was entitled immediately prior to the effective date of that amendment or revision.

Section 33. Certification, Recordation and Deposit of Amendments and Revised Charter—Judicial Notice

Copies of any new or revised charter of the city of St. Louis or of any amendments to the present, or to any new or revised charter, with a certificate thereto appended, signed by the chief executive and authenticated by the seal of the city, setting forth the submission to and ratification thereof, by the qualified voters of the city shall be made in duplicate, one of which shall be deposited in the office of the secretary of state, and the other, after being recorded in the office of the recorder of deeds of the city, shall be deposited among the archives of the city, and thereafter all courts of this state shall take judicial notice thereof.

ARTICLE VII: PUBLIC OFFICERS

Section 1. Impeachment—Officers Liable—Grounds

All elective executive officials of the state, and judges of the supreme court, courts of appeals and circuit courts shall be liable to impeachment for crimes, misconduct, habitual drunkenness, willful neglect of duty, corruption in office, incompetency, or any offense involving moral turpitude or oppression in office.

Section 2. Power of Impeachment—Trial of Impeachments

The house of representatives shall have the sole power of impeachment. All impeachments shall be tried before the supreme court, except that the governor or a member of the supreme court shall be tried by a special commission of seven eminent jurists to be elected by the senate. The supreme court or special commission shall take an oath to try impartially the person impeached, and no person shall be convicted without the concurrence of five-sevenths of the court or special commission.

Section 3. Effect of judgment of impeachment

Judgment of impeachment shall not extend beyond removal from office, but shall not prevent punishment of such officer by the courts on charges growing out of the same matter.

Section 4. Removal of Officers Not Subject to Impeachment

Except as provided in this constitution, all officers not subject to impeachment shall be subject to removal from office in the manner and for the causes provided by law.

Section 5. Election Contests—Executive State Officers—Other Election Con Tests

Contested elections for governor, lieutenant governor and other executive state officers shall be had before the supreme court in the manner provided by law, and the court may appoint one or more commissioners to hear the testimony. The trial and determination of contested elections of all other public officers in the state, shall be by courts of law, or by one or more of the judges thereof. The general assembly shall designate by general law the court or judge by whom the several classes of election contests shall be tried and regulate the manner of trial and all matters incident thereto; but no law assigning jurisdiction or regulating its exercise shall apply to the contest of any election held before the law takes effect.

Section 6. Penalty for nepotism

Any public officer or employee in this state who by virtue of his office or employment names or appoints to public office or employment any relative within the fourth degree, by consanguinity or affinity, shall thereby forfeit his office or employment.

Section 7. Appointment of Officers

Except as provided in this constitution, the appointment of all officers shall be made as prescribed by law.

Section 8. Qualifications for Public Office—Nonresidents

No person shall be elected or appointed to any civil or military office in this state who is not a citizen of the United States, and who shall not have resided in this state one year next preceding his election or appointment, except that the residence in this state shall not be necessary in cases of appointment to administrative positions requiring technical or specialized skill or knowledge.

Section 9. Disqualification by Federal Employment—Exceptions

No person holding an office of profit under the United States shall hold any office of profit in this state, members of the organized militia or of the reserve corps excepted.

Section 10. Equality of Sexes in Public Service

No person shall be disqualified from holding office in this state because of sex.

Section 11. Oath of Office

Before taking office, all civil and military officers in this state shall take and subscribe an oath or affirmation to support the Constitution of the United States and of this state, and to demean themselves faithfully in office.

Section 12. Tenure of Office

Except as provided in this constitution, and subject to the right of resignation, all officers shall hold office for the term thereof, and until their successors are duly elected or appointed and qualified.

Section 13. Limitation On Increase of Compensation and Extension of Terms of Office

The compensation of state, county and municipal officers shall not be increased during the term of office; nor shall the term of any officer be extended.

Section 14. Statement of Actuary Required Before Retirement Benefits Substantially Changed

The legislative body which stipulates by law the amount and type of retirement benefits to be paid by a retirement plan covering elected or appointed public officials or both, shall, before taking final action of any substantial proposed change in future benefits, cause to be prepared a statement regarding the cost of such change. Such statement of cost shall be prepared by a qualified actuary with experience in retirement plan financing and such statement shall be available for public inspection. The general assembly shall provide by law applicable standards and requirements governing the preparation, content, and disposition of such statements of cost.

ARTICLE VIII: SUFFRAGE AND ELECTION

Section 1. Time of General Elections

The general election shall be held on the Tuesday next following the first Monday in November of each even year, unless a different day is fixed by law, two-thirds of all members of each house assenting.

Section 2. Qualifications of Voters—Disqualifications

All citizens of the United States, including occupants of soldiers' and sailors' homes, over the age of eighteen who are residents of this state and of the political subdivision in which they offer to vote are entitled to vote at all elections by the people, if the election is one for which registration is required if they are registered within the time prescribed by law, or if the election is one for which registration is not required, if they have been residents of the political subdivision in which they offer to vote for thirty days next preceding the election for which they offer to vote: Provided however, no person who has a guardian of his or her estate or person by reason of mental incapacity, appointed by a court of competent jurisdiction and no person who is involuntarily confined in a mental institution pursuant to an adjudication of a court of competent jurisdiction shall be entitled to vote, and persons convicted of felony, or crime connected with the exercise of the right of suffrage may be excluded by law from voting.

Section 3. Methods of Voting—Secrecy of Ballot—Exceptions

All elections by the people shall be by ballot or by any mechanical method prescribed by law. All election officers shall be sworn or affirmed not to disclose how any voter voted; provided, that in cases of contested elections, grand jury investigations and in the trial of all civil or criminal cases in which the violation of any law relating to elections, including nominating elections, is under investigation or at issue, such officers may be required to testify and the ballots cast may be opened, examined, counted, and received as evidence.

Section 4. Privilege of Voters From Arrest—Exceptions

Voters shall be privileged from arrest while going to, attending and returning from elections, except in cases of treason, felony or breach of the peace.

Section 5. Registration of Voters

Registration of voters may be provided for by law.

Section 6. Retention of Residence for Voting Purposes

for the purpose of voting, no person shall be deemed to have gained or lost a residence by reason of his presence or absence while engaged in the civil or military service of this state or of the United States, or in the navigation of the high seas or the waters of the state or of the United States, or while a student of any institution of learning, or kept in a poor house or other asylum at public expense, or confined in public prison.

Section 7. Absentee Voting

Qualified electors of the state who are absent, whether within or without the state, may be enabled by general law to vote at all elections by the people.

Section 15. Preamble

The people of Missouri hereby state our intention that this initiative lead to the adoption of the following U.S. Constitutional Amendment.

Section 16. Congressional Term Limits Amendment

(a) No person shall serve in the office of United States Representative for more than three terms, but upon ratification of this amendment no person who has held the office of the United States Representative or who then holds the office shall serve for more than two additional terms.

(b) No person shall serve in the office of United States Senator for more than two terms, but upon ratification of this amendment no person who has held the office of United States Senator or who then holds the office shall serve in the office for more than one additional term.

(c) Any state may enact by state constitutional amendment longer or shorter limits than those specified in section "a" or "b" herein.

(d) This article shall have no time limit within which it must be ratified to become operative upon the ratification of the legislatures of three-fourths of the several States. Therefore, We, the people of the State of Missouri, have chosen to amend the state constitution to inform voters regarding incumbent and non-incumbent federal candidates' support for the above proposed CONGRESSIONAL TERM LIMITS AMENDMENT.

Section 17. Voter Instruction On Term Limits for Members of Congress

(1) We, the Voters of Missouri, hereby instruct each member of our congressional delegation to use all of his or her delegated powers to pass the Congressional Term Limits Amendment set forth above.

(2) All primary and general election ballots shall have printed the information "DISREGARDED VOTERS' INSTRUCTION ON TERM LIMITS" adjacent to the name of any United States Senator or Representative who:

(a) fails to vote in favor of the proposed Congressional Term Limits Amendment set forth above when brought to a vote or;

(b) fails to second the proposed Congressional Term Limits Amendment set forth above if it lacks for a second before any proceeding of the legislative body or;

(c) fails to propose or otherwise bring to a vote of the full legislative body the proposed Congressional Term Limits Amendment set forth above if it otherwise lacks a legislator who so proposes or brings to a vote of the full legislative body the proposed Congressional Term Limits Amendment set forth above or;

(d) fails to vote in favor of all votes bringing the proposed Congressional Term Limits Amendment set forth above before any committee or subcommittee of the respective house upon which he or she serves or;

(e) fails to reject any attempt to delay, table or otherwise prevent a vote by the full legislative body of the proposed Congressional Term Limits Amendment set forth above or;

(f) fails to vote against any proposed constitutional amendment that would establish longer term limits than those in the proposed Congressional Term Limits Amendment set forth above regardless of any other actions in support of the proposed Congressional Term Limits Amendment set forth above, or;

(g) sponsors or cosponsors any proposed constitutional amendment or law that would increase term limits beyond those in the proposed Congressional Term Limits Amendment set forth above, or;

(h) fails to ensure that all votes on Congressional Term Limits are recorded and made available to the public.

(3) The information "DISREGARDED VOTERS' INSTRUCTION ON TERM LIMITS" shall not appear adjacent to the names of incumbent candidates for Congress if the Congressional Term Limits Amendment set forth above is before the states for ratification or has become part of the United States Constitution.

Section 18. Voter Instruction On Term Limit Pledge for Non-Incumbents

(1) Non-incumbent candidates for United States Senator and Representative shall be given an opportunity to take a "Term Limit" pledge regarding "Term Limits" each time they file to run for such office. Those who decline to take the "Term Limits" pledge shall have the information "DECLINED TO PLEDGE TO SUPPORT TERM LIMITS" printed adjacent to their name on every primary and general election ballot.

(2) The "Term Limits" pledge shall be offered to non-incumbent candidates for United States Senator and Representative until a Constitutional Amendment which limits the number of terms of United States Senators to no more than two and United States Representatives to no more than three shall have become part of our United States Constitution.

(3) The "Term Limits" pledge that each non-incumbent candidate, set forth above, shall be offered is as follows: I support term limits and pledge to use all my legislative powers to enact the proposed Constitutional Amendment set forth in the Term Limits Act of 1996. If elected, I pledge to vote in such a way that the designation "DISREGARDED VOTERS' INSTRUCTION ON TERM LIMITS" will not appear adjacent to my name.

Section 19. Designation

(1) The Secretary of State shall be responsible to make an accurate determination as to whether a candidate for the federal legislature shall have placed adjacent to his or her name on the election ballot the information "DISREGARDED VOTERS' INSTRUCTION ON TERM LIMITS" or "DECLINED TO PLEDGE TO SUPPORT TERM LIMITS."

(2) The Secretary of State shall consider timely submitted public comments prior to making the determination required in subsection (1) of this section and may rely on such comments and any information submitted by the candidates in making the determination required in subsection (1).

(3) The Secretary of State, in accordance with subsection (1) of this section shall determine and declare what information, if any, shall appear adjacent to the names of each incumbent federal legislator if he or she was to be a candidate in the next election. This determination and declaration shall be made in a fashion necessary to ensure the orderly printing of primary and general election ballots with allowance made for all legal action provided in section (5) and (6) below, and shall be based upon each member of Congress's action during their current term of office and any action taken in any concluded term, if such action was taken after the determination and declaration was made by the Secretary of State in a previous election.

(4) The Secretary of State shall determine and declare what information, if any, will appear adjacent to the names of non-incumbent candidates for the federal legislature, not later than five (5) business days after the deadline for filing for the office.

(5) If the Secretary of State makes the determination that the information "DISREGARDED VOTERS' INSTRUCTION ON TERM LIMITS" or "DECLINED TO PLEDGE TO SUPPORT TERM LIMITS" shall not be placed on the ballot adjacent to the name of a candidate for the federal legislature, any elector may appeal such decision within five (5) business days to the Missouri Supreme Court as an original action or shall waive any right to appeal such decision; in which case the burden of proof shall be upon the Secretary of State to demonstrate by clear and convincing evidence that the candidate has met the requirements set forth in the Act and therefore should not have the information "DISREGARDED VOTERS' INSTRUCTION ON TERM LIMITS" or "DECLINED TO PLEDGE TO SUPPORT TERM LIMITS" printed on the ballot adjacent to the candidate's name.

(6) If the Secretary of State determines that the information "DISREGARDED VOTERS' INSTRUCTION ON TERM LIMITS" or "DE CLINED TO PLEDGE TO SUPPORT TERM LIMITS" shall be placed on the ballot adjacent to a candidate's name, the candidate may appeal such decision within five (5) business days to the Missouri Supreme Court as an original action or shall waive any right to appeal such decision; in which case the burden of proof shall be upon the candidate to demonstrate by clear and convincing evidence that he or she should not have the information "DISREGARDED VOTERS' INSTRUCTION ON TERM LIMITS" or "DE CLINED TO PLEDGE TO SUPPORT TERM LIMITS" printed on the ballot adjacent to the candidate's name.

(7) The Supreme Court shall hear the appeal provided for in subsection (5) and issue a decision within 60 days. The Supreme Court shall hear the appeal provided for in subsection (6) and issue a decision not later than 61 days before the date of the election.

Section 20. Automatic Repeal

At such time as the Congressional Term Limits Amendment set forth above has become part of the U.S. Constitution, section 15 through section 22 of this Article automatically shall be repealed.

Section 21. Jurisdiction

Any legal challenge to this Amendment shall be filed as an original action before the Supreme Court of this State.

Section 22. Severability

If any portion, clause, or phrase of this Amendment is, for any reason, held to be invalid or unconstitutional by a court of competent jurisdiction, the remaining portions, clauses, and phrases shall not be affected, but shall remain in full force and effect.

ARTICLE IX: EDUCATION

Section 1(A). Free Public Schools—Age Limit

A general diffusion of knowledge and intelligence being essential to the preservation of the rights and liberties of the people, the general assembly shall establish and maintain free public schools for the gratuitous instruction of all persons in this state within ages not in excess of twenty-one years as prescribed by law.

Section 1(B). Specific Schools—Adult Education

Specific schools for any contiguous territory may be established by law. Adult education may be provided from funds other than ordinary school revenues.

Section 2(A). State Board of Education—Number and Appointment of Members—Political Affiliation—Terms—Reimbursement and Compensation

The supervision of instruction in the public schools shall be vested in a state board of education, consisting of eight lay members appointed by the governor, by and with the advice and consent of the senate; provided, that at no time shall more than four members be of the same political party. The term of office of each member shall be eight years, except the terms of the first appointees shall be from one to eight years, respectively. While attending to the duties of their office, members shall be entitled to receive only actual expenses incurred, and a per diem fixed by law.

Section 2(B). Commissioner of Education—Qualification, Duties and Compensation—Appointment and Compensation of Professional Staff—Powers and Duties of State Board of Education

The board shall select and appoint a commissioner of education as its chief administrative officer, who shall be a citizen and resident of the state, and removable at its discretion. The board shall prescribe his duties and fix his compensation, and upon his recommendation shall appoint the professional staff and fix their compensation. The board shall succeed the state board of education heretofore established, with all its powers and duties, and shall have such other powers and duties as may be prescribed by law.

Section 3(A). Payment and Distribution of Appropriations and Income

All appropriations by the state for the support of free public schools and the income from the public school fund shall be paid at least annually and distributed according to law.

Section 3(B). Deficiency in Provision for Eight-Month School Year—Allotment of State Revenue for School Purposes

in event the public school fund provided and set apart by law for the support of free public schools, shall be insufficient to sustain free schools at least eight months in every year in each school district of the state, the general assembly may provide for such deficiency; but in no case shall there be set apart less than twenty-five percent of the state revenue, exclusive of interest and sinking fund, to be applied annually to the support of the free public schools.

Section 3(C). Racial Discrimination in Employment of Teachers

No school district which permits differences in wages of teachers having the same training and experience because of race or color, shall receive any portion of said revenue or fund. Section 4. Public school and seminary funds—certificates of indebtedness—renewals—liquidation—legal investment of funds—tax levy for interest.—All certificates of indebtedness of the state to the public school fund and to the seminary fund are hereby confirmed as sacred obligations of the state to said funds, and they shall be renewed as they mature for such time and at such rate of interest as may be provided by law. The general assembly may provide at any time for the liquidation of said certificates, but all funds derived from such liquidation, and all other funds hereafter accruing to said state school or state seminary funds, except the interest on same, shall be invested only in registered bonds of the United States or the state, bonds of school districts of the state, or bonds or other securities payment of which are fully guaranteed by the United States, of not less than par value. The general assembly may levy an annual tax sufficient to pay the accruing interest of all state certificates of indebtedness.

Section 5. Public School Fund—Sources—Payment Into State Treasury—Investment—Limitation On Use of Income

The proceeds of all certificates of indebtedness due the state school fund, and all moneys, bonds, lands, and other property belonging to or donated to any state fund for public school purposes, and the net proceeds of all sales of lands and other property and effects that may accrue to the state by escheat, shall be paid into the state treasury, and securely invested under the supervision of the state board of education, and sacredly preserved as a public school fund the annual income of which shall be faithfully appropriated for establishing and maintaining free public schools, and for no other uses or purposes whatsoever.

Section 6. Seminary Fund—Sources—Payment Into State Treasury—Investment—Limitation On Use of Income

The proceeds of all certificates of indebtedness due the seminary fund, the net proceeds of all sales of lands granted to the state for the benefit of the state university with its several divisions, as provided by law, and all gifts, grants, bequests, or devises to said seminary fund for the benefit of the university, and not otherwise appropriated by the terms of any such gift, grant, bequest or devise, shall be paid into the state treasury, and securely invested by the board of curators of the state university and sacredly preserved as a seminary fund, the annual income of which shall be faithfully appropriated for maintenance of the state university, and for no other uses or purposes whatsoever.

Section 7. County and Township School Funds—Liquidation and Reinvestment— Optional Distribution On Liquidation—Annual Distribution of Income and Receipts

All real estate, loans, and investments now belonging to the various county and township school funds, except those invested as hereinafter provided, shall be liquidated without extension of time, and the proceeds thereof and the money on hand now belonging to said school funds of the several counties and the city of St. Louis, shall be reinvested in registered bonds of the United States, or in bonds of the state or in approved bonds of any city or school district thereof, or in bonds or other securities the payment of which are fully guaranteed by the United States, and sacredly preserved as a county school fund. Any county or the city of St. Louis by a majority vote of the qualified electors voting thereon may elect to distribute annually to its schools the proceeds of the liquidated school fund, at the time and in the manner prescribed by law. All interest accruing from investment of the county school fund, the clear proceeds of all penalties, forfeitures and fines collected hereafter for any breach of the penal laws of the state, the net proceeds from the sale of estrays, and all other moneys coming into said funds shall be distributed annually to the schools of the several counties according to law.

Section 8. Prohibition of Public Aid for Religious Purposes and Institutions

Neither the general assembly, nor any county, city, town, township, school district or other municipal corporation, shall ever make an appropriation or pay from any public fund whatever, anything in aid of any religious creed, church or sectarian purpose, or to help to support or sustain any private or public school, academy, seminary, college, university, or other institution of learning controlled by any religious creed, church or sectarian denomination whatever; nor shall any grant or donation of personal property or real estate ever be made by the state, or any county, city, town, or other municipal corporation, for any religious creed, church, or sectarian purpose whatever.

Section 9(A). State University—Government by Board of Curators—Number and Appointment

The government of the state university shall be vested in a board of curators consisting of nine members appointed by the governor, by and with the advice and consent of the senate.

Section 9(B). Maintenance of State University and Other Educational Institutions

The general assembly shall adequately maintain the state university and such other educational institutions as it may deem necessary.

Section 10. Free Public Libraries—Declaration of Policy—State Aid to Local Public Libraries

It is hereby declared to be the policy of the state to promote the establishment and development of free public libraries and to accept the obligation of their support by the state and its subdivisions and municipalities in such manner as may be provided by law. When any such subdivision or municipality supports a free library, the general assembly shall grant aid to such public library in such manner and in such amounts as may be provided by law.

ARTICLE X: TAXATION

Section 1. Taxing Power—Exercise by State and Local Governments

The taxing power may be exercised by the general assembly for state purposes, and by counties and other political subdivisions under power granted to them by the general assembly for county, municipal and other corporate purposes.

Section 2. Inalienability of Power to Tax

The power to tax shall not be surrendered, suspended or contracted away, except as authorized by this constitution.

Section 3. Limitation of Taxation to Public Purposes—Uniformity—General Laws—Time for Payment of Taxes—Valuation

Taxes may be levied and collected for public purposes only, and shall be uniform upon the same class or subclass of subjects within the territorial limits of the authority levying the tax. All taxes shall be levied and collected by general laws and shall be payable during the fiscal or calendar year in which the property is assessed. Except as otherwise provided in this constitution, the methods of determining the value of property for taxation shall be fixed by law.

Section 4(A). Classification of Taxable Property—Taxes On Franchises, Incomes, Excises and Licenses

All taxable property shall be classified for tax purposes as follows: class 1, real property; class 2, tangible personal property; class 3, intangible personal property. The general assembly, by general law, may provide for further classification within classes 2 and 3, based solely on the nature and characteristics of the property, and not on the nature, residence or business of the owner, or the amount owned. Nothing in this section shall prevent the taxing of franchises, privileges or incomes, or the levying of excise or motor vehicle license taxes, or any other taxes of the same or different types.

Section 4(B). Basis of Assessment of Tangible Property—Real Property—Taxation of Intangibles—Limitations

Property in classes 1 and 2 and subclasses of those classes, shall be assessed for tax purposes at its value or such percentage of its value as may be fixed by law for each class and for each subclass. Property in class 3 and its subclasses shall be taxed only to the extent authorized and at the rate fixed by law for each class and subclass, and the tax shall be based on the annual yield and shall not exceed eight percent thereof. Property in class 1 shall be subclassed in the following classifications:

(1) Residential property;

(2) Agricultural and horticultural property;

(3) Utility, industrial, commercial, railroad, and all other property not included in subclasses (1) and (2) of class 1. Property in the subclasses of class 1 may be defined by law, however subclasses (1), (2), and (3) shall not be further divided, provided, land in subclass (2) may by general law be assessed for tax purposes on its productive capability. The same percentage of value shall be applied to all properties within any subclass. No classes or subclass shall have a percentage of its true value in money in excess of thirty-three and one-third percent.

Section 4(C). Assessment, Levy, Collection and Distribution of Tax On Intangibles

All taxes on property in class 3 and its subclasses, and the tax under any other form of taxation substituted by the general assembly for the tax on bank shares, shall be assessed, levied and collected by the state and returned as provided by law, less two percent for collection, to the counties and other political subdivisions of their origin, in proportion to the respective local rates of levy.

Section 4(D). Income Tax Laws, May Incorporate Federal Laws by Reference— Rates, How Set

in enacting any law imposing a tax on or measured by income, the general assembly may define income by reference to provisions of the laws of the United States as they may be or become effective at any time or from time to time, whether retrospective or prospective in their operation. The general assembly shall in any such law set the rate or rates of such tax. The general assembly may in so defining income make exceptions, additions, or modifications to any provisions of the laws of the United States so referred to and for retrospective exceptions or modifications to those provisions which are retrospective.

Section 5. Taxation of Railroads

All railroad corporations in this state, or doing business therein, shall be subject to taxation for state, county, school, municipal and other purposes, on the real and personal property owned or used by them, and on their gross earnings, their net earnings, their franchises and their capital stock.

Section 6. Property Exempt From Taxation

1. All property, real and personal, of the state, counties and other political subdivisions, and nonprofit cemeteries, and all real property used as a homestead as defined by law of any citizen of this state who is a former prisoner of war, as defined by law, and who has a total service-connected disability, shall be exempt from taxation; all personal property held as industrial inventories, including raw materials, work in progress and finished work on hand, by manufacturers and refiners, and all personal property held as goods, wares, merchandise, stock in trade or inventory for resale by distributors, wholesalers, or retail merchants or establishments shall be exempt from taxation; and all property, real and personal, not held for private or corporate profit and used exclusively for religious worship, for schools and colleges, for purposes purely charitable, for agricultural and horticultural societies, or for veterans' organizations may be exempted from taxation by general law. in addition to the above, household goods, furniture, wearing apparel and articles of personal use and adornment owned and used by a person in his home or dwelling place may be exempt from taxation by general law but any such law may provide for approximate restitution to the respective political subdivisions of revenues lost by reason of the exemption. All laws exempting from taxation property other than the property enumerated in this article, shall be void. The provisions of this section exempting certain personal property of manufacturers, refiners, distributors, wholesalers, and retail merchants and establishments from taxation shall become effective, unless otherwise provided by law, in each county on January 1 of the year in which that county completes its first general reassessment as defined by law.

2. All revenues lost because of the exemption of certain personal property of manufacturers, refiners, distributors, wholesalers, and retail merchants and establishments shall be replaced to each taxing authority within a county from a countywide tax hereby imposed on all property in subclass 3 of class 1 in each county. for the year in which the exemption becomes effective, the county clerk shall calculate the total revenue lost by all taxing authorities in the county and extend upon all property in subclass 3 of class 1 within the county, a tax at the rate necessary to produce that amount. The rate of tax levied in each county according to this subsection shall not be increased above the rate first imposed and will stand levied at that rate unless later reduced according to the provisions of subsection 3. The county collector shall disburse the proceeds according to the revenue lost by each taxing authority because of the exemption of such property in that county. Restitution of the revenues lost by any taxing district contained in more than one county shall be from the several counties according to the revenue lost because of the exemption of property in each county. Each year after the first year the replacement tax is imposed, the amount distributed to each taxing authority in a county shall be increased or decreased by an amount equal to the amount resulting from the change in that district's total assessed value of property in subclass 3 of class 1 at the countywide replacement tax rate. in order to implement the provisions of this subsection, the limits set in section 11(b) of this article may be exceeded, without voter approval, if necessary to allow each county listed in section 11(b) to comply with this subsection.

3. Any increase in the tax rate imposed pursuant to subsection 2 of this section shall be decreased if such decrease is approved by a majority of the voters of the county voting on such decrease. A decrease in the increased tax rate imposed under subsection 2 of this section may be submitted to the voters of a county by the governing body thereof upon its own order, ordinance, or resolution and shall be submitted upon the petition of at least eight percent of the qualified voters who voted in the immediately preceding gubernatorial election.

4. As used in this section, the terms "revenues lost" and "lost revenues" shall mean that revenue which each taxing authority received from the imposition of a tangible personal property tax on all personal property held as industrial inventories, including raw materials, work in progress and finished work on hand, by manufacturers and refiners, and all personal property held as goods, wares, merchandise, stock in trade or inventory for resale by distributors, wholesalers, or retail merchants or establishments in the last full tax year immediately preceding the effective date of the exemption from taxation granted for such property under subsection 1 of this section, and which was no longer received after such exemption became effective.

Section 6(A). Homestead Exemption Authorized

The general assembly may provide that a portion of the assessed valuation of real property actually occupied by the owner or owners thereof as a homestead, be exempted from the payment of taxes thereon, in such amounts and upon such conditions as may be determined by law, and the general assembly may provide for certain tax credits or rebates in lieu of or in addition to such an exemption, but any such law shall further provide for restitution to the respective political subdivisions of revenues lost, if any, by reason of the exemption, and any such law may also provide for comparable financial relief to persons who are not the owners of homesteads but who occupy rental property as their homes.

Section 6(B). Intangible Property Exempt From Taxation, When—Local Governments May be Reimbursed, When

The general assembly may by general law exempt from taxation all intangible property, including taxation on the yield thereof, when owned by:

(1) Individuals; or

(2) Labor, agricultural or horticultural organizations; or

(3) Corporations or associations organized and operated exclusively for religious, charitable, scientific or educational purposes, no part of the net in come of which inures to the benefit of any private stockholder or individual; or

(4) Hospitals which are exempt from payment of Missouri state income tax. Any such law may provide for approximate reimbursement to the various political subdivisions, by the state, of revenues lost because of the exemption.

Section 7. Relief From Taxation—Forest Lands—Obsolete, Decadent, Or Blighted Areas—Limitations—Exception

for the purpose of encouraging forestry when lands are devoted exclusively to such purpose, and the reconstruction, redevelopment, and rehabilitation of obsolete, decadent, or blighted areas, the general assembly by general law may provide for such partial relief from taxation of the lands devoted to any such purpose, and of the improvements thereon, by such method or methods, for such period or periods of time, not exceeding twenty-five years in any instance, and upon such terms, conditions, and restrictions as it may prescribe; provided, however, that in the case of forest lands, the limitation of twenty-five years herein described shall not apply.

Section 8. Limitation On State Tax Rate On Tangible Property

The state tax on real and tangible personal property, exclusive of the tax necessary to pay any bonded debt of the state, shall not exceed ten cents on the hundred dollars assessed valuation.

Section 9. Immunity of Private Property From Sale for Municipal Debts

Private property shall not be taken or sold for the payment of the corporate debt of a municipal corporation.

Section 10(A). Exclusion of State From Local Taxation for Local Purposes.

Except as provided in this constitution, the general assembly shall not impose taxes upon counties or other political subdivisions or upon the inhabitants or property thereof for municipal, county or other corporate purposes.

Section 10(B). State Aid for Local Purposes

Nothing in this constitution shall prevent the enactment of general laws directing the payment of funds collected for state purposes to counties or other political subdivisions as state aid for local purposes.

Section 10(C). Reduction in Rates of Levy May be Required by Law

The general assembly may require by law that political subdivisions reduce the rate of levy of all property taxes the subdivisions impose whether the rate of levy is authorized by this constitution or by law. The general assembly may by law establish the method of increasing reduced rates of levy in subsequent years.

Section 11(A). Taxing Jurisdiction of Local Governments—Limitation On Assessed Valuation

Taxes may be levied by counties and other political subdivisions on all property subject to their taxing power, but the assessed valuation therefor in such other political subdivisions shall not exceed the assessed valuation of the same property for state and county purposes.

Section 11(B). Limitations On Local Tax Rates

Any tax imposed upon such property by municipalities, counties or school districts, for their respective purposes, shall not exceed the following annual rates: for municipalities—one dollar on the hundred dollars assessed valuation; for counties—thirty-five cents on the hundred dollars assessed valuation in counties having three hundred million dollars, or more, assessed valuation and having by operation of law attained the classification of a county of the first class; and fifty cents on the hundred dollars assessed valuation in all other counties; for school districts formed of cities and towns, including the school district of the city of St. Louis—two dollars and seventy-five cents on the hundred dollars assessed valuation; for all other school districts—sixty-five cents on the hundred dollars assessed valuation.

Section 11(C). Increase of Tax Rate by Popular Vote—Further Limitation by Law—Exceptions to Limitation

in all municipalities, counties and school districts the rates of taxation as herein limited may be increased for their respective purposes when the rate and purpose of the increase are submitted to a vote and two-thirds of the qualified electors voting thereon shall vote therefor; provided in school districts the rate of taxation as herein limited may be increased for school purposes so that the total levy shall not exceed six dollars on the hundred dollars assessed valuation, except as herein provided, when the rate and the purpose of the increase are submitted to a vote and a majority of the qualified electors voting thereon shall vote therefor; provided, that in any school district where the board of education is not proposing a higher tax rate for school purposes, the last tax rate approved shall continue and the tax rate need not be submitted to the voters; provided, that in school districts where the qualified voters have voted against a proposed higher tax rate for school purposes, then the rate shall remain at the rate approved in the last previous school election except that the board of education shall be free to resubmit any higher tax rate at any time; provided that any board of education may levy a lower tax rate than approved by the voters as authorized by any provision of this section; and provided, that the rates herein fixed, and the amounts by which they may be increased may be further limited by law; and provided further, that any county or other political subdivision, when authorized by law and within the limits fixed by law, may levy a rate of taxation on all property subject to its taxing powers in excess of the rates herein limited, for library, hospital, public health, recreation grounds and museum purposes.

Section 11(D). Tax Rate in St. Louis for County Purposes

The city of St. Louis may levy for county purposes, in addition to the municipal rates herein provided, a rate not exceeding the rate allowed for county purposes.

Section 11(E). Exclusion of Bonded Debt From Limitations On Tax Rates

The foregoing limitations on rates shall not apply to taxes levied for the purpose of paying any bonded debt.

Section 11(F). Authorization of Local Taxes Other Than Ad Valorem Taxes

Nothing in this constitution shall prevent the enactment of any general law permitting any county or other political subdivision to levy taxes other than ad valorem taxes for its essential purposes.

Section 11(G). Operating Levy for Kansas City School Districts May be Set by School Board

The school board of any school district whose operating levy for school purposes for the 1995 tax year was established pursuant to a federal court order may establish the operating levy for school purposes for the district at a rate that is lower than the court-ordered rate for the 1995 tax year. The rate so established may be changed from year to year by the school board of the district. Approval by a majority of the voters of the district voting thereon shall be required for any operating levy for school purposes equal to or greater than the rate established by court order for the 1995 tax year. The authority granted in this section shall apply to any successor school district or successor school districts of such school district.

Section 12(A). Additional Tax Rates for County Roads and Bridges—Road Districts—Reduction in Rate May be Required, How

in addition to the rates authorized in section 11 for county purposes, the county court in the several counties not under township organization, the township board of directors in the counties under township organization, and the proper administrative body in counties adopting an alternative form of government, may levy an additional tax, not exceeding fifty cents on each hundred dollars assessed valuation, all of such tax to be collected and turned in to the county treasury to be used for road and bridge purposes; provided that, before any such county may increase its tax levy for road and bridge purposes above thirty-five cents it must submit such increase to the qualified voters of that county at a general or special election and receive the approval of a majority of the voters voting on such increase. in addition to the above levy for road and bridge purposes, it shall be the duty of the county court, when so authorized by a majority of the qualified electors of any road district, general or special, voting thereon at an election held for such purpose, to make an additional levy of not to exceed thirty-five cents on the hundred dollars assessed valuation on all taxable real and tangible personal property within such district, to be collected in the same manner as state and county taxes, and placed to the credit of the road district authorizing such levy, such election to be called and held in the manner provided by law provided that the general assembly may require by law that the rates authorized herein may be reduced.

Section 12(B). Refund of Road and Bridge Taxes

Nothing in this section shall prevent the refund of taxes collected hereunder to cities and towns for road and bridge purposes.

Section 13. Tax Sales—Limitations—Contents of Notices

No real property shall be sold for state, county or city taxes without judicial proceedings, unless the notice of sale shall contain the names of all record owners thereof, or the names of all owners appearing on the land tax book, and all other information required by law.

Section 14. Equalization Commission—Appointment—Duties

The general assembly shall establish a commission, to be appointed by the governor by and with the advice and consent of the senate, to equalize assessments as between counties and, under such rules as may be prescribed by law, to hear appeals from local boards in individual cases and, upon such appeal, to correct any assessment which is shown to be unlawful, unfair, arbitrary or capricious. Such commission shall perform all other duties prescribed by law.

Section 15. Definition of "other Political Subdivision"

The term "other political subdivision," as used in this article, shall be construed to include townships, cities, towns, villages, school, road, drainage, sewer and levee districts and any other public subdivision, public corporation or public quasi-corporation having the power to tax. Section 16. Taxes and state spending to be limited—state to support certain local activities—emergency spending and bond payments to be authorized.— Property taxes and other local taxes and state taxation and spending may not be increased above the limitations specified herein without direct voter approval as provided by this constitution. The state is prohibited from requiring any new or expanded activities by counties and other political subdivisions without full state financing, or from shifting the tax burden to counties and other political subdivisions. A provision for emergency conditions is established and the repayment of voter approved bonded indebtedness is guaranteed. Implementation of this section is specified in sections 17 through 24, inclusive, of this article.

Section 17. Definitions

As used in sections 16 through 24 of Article X:

(1) "Total state revenues" includes all general and special revenues, license and fees, excluding federal funds, as defined in the budget message of the governor for fiscal year 1980-1981. Total state revenues shall exclude the amount of any credits based on actual tax liabilities or the imputed tax components of rental payments, but shall include the amount of any credits not related to actual tax liabilities.

(2) "Personal income of Missouri" is the total income received by persons in Missouri from all sources, as defined and officially reported by the United States Department of Commerce or its successor agency.

(3) "General price level" means the Consumer Price Index for All Urban Consumers for the United States, or its successor publications, as defined and officially reported by the United States Department of Labor, or its successor agency.

Section 18. Limitation On Taxes Which May be Imposed by General Assembly— Exclusions—Refund of Excess Revenue—Adjustments Authorized

(a) There is hereby established a limit on the total amount of taxes which may be imposed by the general assembly in any fiscal year on the taxpayers of this state. Effective with fiscal year 1981-1982, and for each fiscal year thereafter, the general assembly shall not impose taxes of any kind which, together with all other revenues of the state, federal funds excluded, exceed the revenue limit established in this section. The revenue limit shall be calculated for each fiscal year and shall be equal to the product of the ratio of total state revenues in fiscal year 1980-1981 divided by the personal income of Missouri in calendar year

1979 multiplied by the personal income of Missouri in either the calendar year prior to the calendar year in which appropriations for the fiscal year for which the calculation is being made, or the average of personal income of Missouri in the previous three calendar years, whichever is greater.

(b) for any fiscal year in the event that total state revenues exceed the revenue limit established in this section by one percent or more, the excess revenues shall be refunded pro rata based on the liability reported on the Missouri state income tax (or its successor tax or taxes) annual returns filed following the close of such fiscal year. If the excess is less than one percent, this excess shall be transferred to the general revenue fund.

(c) The revenue limitation established in this section shall not apply to taxes imposed for the payment of principal and interest on bonds, approved by the voters and authorized under the provisions of this constitution.

(d) If responsibility for funding a program or programs is transferred from one level of government to another, as a consequence of constitutional amendment, the state revenue and spending limits may be adjusted to accommodate such change, provided that the total revenue authorized for collection by both state and local governments does not exceed that amount which would have been authorized without such change.

(e) Voter approval required for taxes or fees, when, exceptions—definitions—compliance procedure, remedies.

1. in addition to the revenue limit imposed by section 18 of this article, the general assembly in any fiscal year shall not increase taxes or fees without voter approval that in total produce new annual revenues greater than either fifty million dollars adjusted annually by the percentage change in the personal income of Missouri for the second previous fiscal year, or one percent of total state revenues for the second fiscal year prior to the general assembly's action, whichever is less. in the event that an individual or series of tax or fee increases exceed the ceiling established in the subsection, the taxes or fees shall be submitted by the general assembly to a public vote starting with the largest increase in the given year, and including all increases in descending order, until the aggregate of the remaining increases and decreases is less than the ceiling provided in this subsection.

2. The term "new annual revenues" means the net increase in annual revenues produced by the total of all tax or fee increases enacted by the general assembly in a fiscal year, less applicable refunds and less all contemporaneously occurring tax or fee reductions in that same fiscal year, and shall not include interest earnings on the proceeds of the tax or fee increase. for purposes of this calculation, "enacted by the general assembly" shall include any and all bills that are truly agreed to and finally passed within that fiscal year, except bills vetoed by the governor and not overridden by the general assembly. Each individual tax or fee increase shall be measured by the estimated new annual revenues collected during the first fiscal year that is fully effective. The term "increase taxes or fees" means any law or laws passed by the general assembly after the effective date of this section that increase the rate of an existing tax or fee, impose a new tax or fee, or broaden the scope of a tax or fee to include additional class of property, activity, or income, but shall not include the extension of an existing tax or fee which was set to expire.

3. in the event of an emergency, the general assembly may increase taxes, licenses or fees for one year beyond the limit in this subsection under the same procedure specified in section 19 of this article.

4. Compliance with the limit in this section shall be measured by calculating the aggregate actual new annual revenues produced in the first fiscal year that each individual tax or fee change is fully effective.

5. Any taxpayer or statewide elected official may bring an action under the provisions of section 23 of this article to enforce compliance with the provisions of this section. The Missouri supreme court shall have original jurisdiction to hear any challenge brought by any statewide elected official to enforce this section. in such enforcement actions, the court shall invalidate the taxes and fees which should have received a public vote as defined in subsection 1 of this section. The court shall order remedies of the amount of revenue collected in excess of the limit in this subsection as the court finds appropriate in order to allow such excess amounts to be refunded or to reduce taxes and/or fees in the future to offset the excess monies collected.

Section 19. Limits May be Exceeded, When, How

The revenue limit of section 18 of this article may be exceeded only if all of the following conditions are met:

(1) The governor requests the general assembly to declare an emergency;

(2) the request is specific as to the nature of the emergency, the dollar amount of the emergency, and the method by which the emergency will be funded; and

(3) the general assembly thereafter declares an emergency in accordance with the specifics of the governor's request by a majority vote for fiscal year 1981-1982, thereafter a two-thirds vote of the members elected to and serving in each house. The emergency must be declared in accordance with this section prior to incurring any of the expenses which constitute the emergency request. The revenue limit may be exceeded only during the fiscal year for which the emergency is declared. in no event shall any part of the amount representing a refund under section 18 of this article be the subject of an emergency request.

Section 20. Limitation On State Expenses

No expenses of state government shall be incurred in any fiscal year which exceed the sum of the revenue limit established in sections 18 and 19 of this article plus federal funds and any surplus from a previous fiscal year. (Adopted November 4, 1980)

Section 21. State Support to Local Governments Not to be Reduced, Additional Activities and Services Not to be Imposed Without Full State Funding

The state is hereby prohibited from reducing the state financed proportion of the costs of any existing activity or service required of counties and other political subdivisions. A new activity or service or an increase in the level of any activity or service beyond that required by existing law shall not be required by the general assembly or any state agency of counties or other political subdivisions, unless a state appropriation is made and disbursed to pay the county or other political subdivision for any increased costs.

Section 22. Political Subdivisions to Receive Voter Approval for Increases in Taxes and Fees—Rollbacks May be Required—Limitation Not Applicable to Taxes for Bonds

(a) Counties and other political subdivisions are hereby prohibited from levying any tax, license or fees, not authorized by law, charter or self-enforcing provisions of the constitution when this section is adopted or from increasing the current levy of an existing tax, license or fees, above that current levy authorized by law or charter when this section is adopted without the approval of the required majority of the qualified voters of that county or other political subdivision voting thereon. If the definition of the base of an existing tax, license or fees, is broadened, the maximum authorized current levy of taxation on the new base in each county or other political subdivision shall be reduced to yield the same estimated gross revenue as on the prior base. If the assessed valuation of property as finally equalized, excluding the value of new construction and improvements, increases by a larger percentage than the increase in the general price level from the previous year, the maximum authorized current levy applied thereto in each county or other political subdivision shall be reduced to yield the same gross revenue from existing property, adjusted for changes in the general price level, as could have been collected at the existing authorized levy on the prior assessed value.

(b) The limitations of this section shall not apply to taxes imposed for the payment of principal and interest on bonds or other evidence of indebtedness or for the payment of assessments on contract obligations in anticipation of which bonds are issued which were authorized prior to the effective date of this section.

Section 23. Taxpayers May Bring Actions for Interpretations of Limitations

Notwithstanding other provisions of this constitution or other law, any taxpayer of the state, county, or other political subdivision shall have standing to bring suit in a circuit court of proper venue and additionally, when the state is involved, in the Missouri supreme court, to enforce the provisions of sections 16 through 22, inclusive, of this article and, if the suit is sustained, shall receive from the applicable unit of government his costs, including reasonable attorneys' fees incurred in maintaining such suit.

Section 24. Voter Approval Requirements Not Exclusive—Self-Enforceability

(a) The provisions for voter approval contained in sections 16 through 23, inclusive, of this article do not abrogate and are in addition to other provisions of the constitution requiring voter approval to incur bonded indebtedness and to authorize certain taxes.

(b) The provisions contained in sections 16 through 23, inclusive, of this article are self-enforcing; provided, however, that the general assembly may enact laws implementing such provisions which are not inconsistent with the purposes of said sections.

Section 25. Sale Or Transfer of Homes Or Other Real Estate, Prohibition On Imposition of Any New Taxes, When

After the effective date of this section, the state, counties, and other political subdivisions are hereby prevented from imposing any new tax, including a sales tax, on the sale or transfer of homes or any other real estate.

ARTICLE XI: CORPORATIONS

Section 1. Definition of "Corporation"

The term "corporation," as used in this article, shall be construed to include all joint stock companies or associations having any powers or privileges not possessed by individuals or partnerships.

Section 2. Organization of Corporations by General Law—Special Laws Relating to Corporations—Invalidation of Unexercised Charters and Franchises

Corporations shall be organized only under general laws. No corporation shall be created, nor shall any existing charter be extended or amended by special law; nor shall any law remit the forfeiture of any charter granted by special act. All existing charters, or grants of special or exclusive privileges, under which a bona fide organization was not completed, and business was not being done in good faith at the adoption of this constitution, shall thereafter have no validity.

Section 3. Exercise of Police Power With Respect to Corporations

The exercise of the police power of the state shall never be surrendered, abridged, or construed to permit corporations to infringe the equal rights of individuals, or the general well-being of the state.

Section 4. Corporations Subject to Eminent Domain—Trial by Jury

The exercise of the power and right of eminent domain shall never be construed or abridged to prevent the taking by law of the property and franchises of corporations and subjecting them to public use. The right of trial by jury shall be held inviolate in all trials of claims for compensation, when the rights of any corporation are affected by any exercise of said power of eminent domain.

Section 5. Repealed

Section 6. Cumulative Voting Authorized Unless Alternate Method Provided by Law—Exceptions

in all elections for directors or managers of any corporation, each shareholder shall have the right to cast as many votes in the aggregate as shall equal the number of shares held by him, multiplied by the number of directors or managers to be elected, and may cast the whole number of votes, either in person or by proxy for one candidate, or distribute such votes among two or more candidates; and such directors or managers shall not be elected in any other manner unless an alternative method of electing and removing directors and managers is adopted as provided by law; provided, that this section shall not apply to cooperative associations, societies or exchanges organized under the law.

Section 7. Consideration for Corporate Stock and Debts— Fictitious Issues— Antecedent Debts—Increases of Stock Or Bonds—Issuance of Preferred Stock

No corporation shall issue stock, or bonds or other obligations for the payment of money, except for money paid, labor done or property actually received; and all fictitious issues or increases of stock or indebtedness shall be void; provided, that no such issue or increase made for valid bona fide antecedent debts shall be deemed fictitious or void. The stock or bonded indebtedness of corporations shall not be increased nor shall preferred stock be issued, except according to general law.

Section 8. Limitation of Liability of Stockholders

No stockholder or subscriber to stock of a corporation shall be individually liable in any amount in excess of the amount originally subscribed on such stock.

RAILROADS

Section 9. Public Highways—Common Carriers—Regulations

All railways in this state are hereby declared public highways, and railroad corporations common carriers. Laws shall be enacted to correct abuses and prevent unjust discrimination and extortion in the rates of freight and passenger tariffs on all railroads in this state.

Section 10. Consolidation of Domestic With Foreign Railroad Corporations— Jurisdiction of Missouri Courts— Notice of Consolidation

If any railroad corporation organized under the laws of this state shall consolidate by sale or otherwise, with any railroad corporation organized under the laws of any other state, or of the United States, the same shall not thereby become a foreign corporation, but the courts of this state shall retain jurisdiction in all matters which may arise as if said consolidation had not taken place. No consolidation shall take place, except upon at least sixty days public notice to all stockholders, in the manner provided by law.

Section 11. Local Consent for Street Railroads

No law shall grant the right to construct and operate a street railroad within any city, town, village, or on any public highway, without first acquiring the consent of the local authorities having control of the street or highway, and the franchises so granted shall not be transferred without similar assent first obtained.

Section 12. Prohibition of Discrimination, Favoritism and Preferences

No discrimination in charges or facilities in transportation shall be made between transportation corporations and individuals, or in favor of either, by abatement, drawback or otherwise; and no common carrier, or any lessee, manager or employee thereof, shall make any preference in furnishing cars or motive power.

BANKS

Section 13. Exclusion of State From Banking

No state bank shall be created, nor shall the state own or be liable for any stock in any corporation, joint stock company, or association for banking purposes.

ARTICLE XII: AMENDING THE CONSTITUTION

Section 1. Limitation On Revision and Amendment

This constitution may be revised and amended only as therein provided.

Section 2(A). Proposal of Amendments by General Assembly

Constitutional amendments may be proposed at any time by a majority of the members-elect of each house of the general assembly, the vote to be taken by yeas and nays and entered on the journal.

Section 2(B). Submission of Amendments Proposed by General Assembly Or by The Initiative

All amendments proposed by the general assembly or by the initiative shall be submitted to the electors for their approval or rejection by official ballot title as may be provided by law, on a separate ballot without party designation, at the next general election, or at a special election called by the governor prior thereto, at which he may submit any of the amendments. No such proposed amendment shall contain more than one amended and revised article of this constitution, or one new article which shall not contain more than one subject and matters properly connected therewith. If possible, each proposed amendment shall be published once a week for two consecutive weeks in two newspapers of different political faith in each county, the last publication to be not more than thirty nor less than fifteen days next preceding the election. If there be but one newspaper in any county, publication for four consecutive weeks shall be made. If a majority of the votes cast thereon is in favor of any amendment, the same shall take effect at the end of thirty days after the election. More than one amendment at the same election shall be so submitted as to enable the electors to vote on each amendment separately.

Section 3(A). Referendum On Constitutional Convention —Qualifications of Delegates—Selection of Nominees for District Delegates and Delegates-At-Large— Election Procedure

At the general election on the first Tuesday following the first Monday in November 1962, and every twenty years thereafter, the secretary of state shall, and at any general or special election the general assembly by law may, submit to the electors of the state the question "Shall there be a convention to revise and amend the constitution?" The question shall be submitted on a separate ballot without party designation, and if a majority of the votes cast thereon is for the affirmative, the governor shall call an election of delegates to the convention on a day not less than three nor more than six months after the election on the question. At the election the electors of the state shall elect fifteen delegates-at-large and the electors of each state senatorial district shall elect two delegates. Each delegate shall possess the qualifications of a senator; and no person holding any other office of trust or profit (officers of the organized militia, school directors, justices of the peace and notaries public excepted) shall be eligible to be elected a delegate. to secure representation from different political parties in each senatorial district, in the manner prescribed by its senatorial district committee each political party shall nominate but one candidate for delegate from each senatorial district, the certificate of nomination shall be filed in the office of the secretary of state at least thirty days before the election, each candidate shall be voted for on a separate ballot bearing the party designation, each elector shall vote for but one of the candidates, and the two candidates receiving the highest number of votes in each senatorial district shall be elected. Candidates for delegates-at-large shall be nominated by nominating petitions only, which shall be signed by electors of the state equal to five percent of the legal voters in the senatorial district in which the candidate resides until otherwise provided by law, and shall be verified as provided by law for initiative petitions, and filed in the office of the secretary of state at least thirty days before the election. All such candidates shall be voted for on a separate ballot without party designation, and the fifteen receiving the highest number of votes shall be elected. Not less than fifteen days before the election, the secretary of state shall certify to the county clerk of the county the name of each person nominated for the office of delegate from the senatorial district in which the county, or any part of it, is included, and the names of all persons nominated for delegates-at-large.

Section 3(B). Convention of Delegates—Quarters—Oath—Compensation— Quorum—Vote Required—Organization, Employees, Printing—Public Sessions— Rules—Vacancies

The delegates so elected shall be convened at the seat of government by proclamation of the governor within six months after their election. The facilities of the legislative chambers and legislative quarters shall be made available for the convention and the delegates. Upon convening all delegates shall take an oath or affirmation to support the Constitution of the United States and of the state of Missouri, and to discharge faithfully their duties as delegates to the convention, and shall receive for their services the sum of ten dollars per diem and mileage as provided by law for members of the general assembly. A majority of the delegates shall constitute a quorum for the transaction of business, and no constitution or amendment to this constitution shall be submitted to the electors for approval or rejection unless by the assent of a majority of all the delegates-elect, the yeas and nays being entered on the journal. The convention may appoint such officers, employees and assistants as it may deem necessary, fix their compensation, provide for the printing of its documents, journals, proceedings and a record of its debates, and appropriate money for the expenditures incurred. The sessions of the convention shall be held with open doors, and it shall determine the rules of its own proceedings, choose its own officers, and be the judge of the election, returns and qualifications of its delegates. in case of a vacancy by death, resignation or other cause, the vacancy shall be filled by the governor by the appointment of another delegate of the political party of the delegate causing the vacancy.

Section 3(C). Submission of Proposal Adopted by Convention—Time of Election—Effective Date

Any proposed constitution or constitutional amendment adopted by the convention shall be submitted to a vote of the electors of the state at such time, in such manner and containing such separate and alternative propositions and on such official ballot as may be provided by the convention, at a special election not less than sixty days nor more than six months after the adjournment of the convention. Upon the approval of the constitution or constitutional amendments the same shall take effect at the end of thirty days after the election. The result of the election shall be proclaimed by the governor.

SCHEDULE

Section 1. Supersession of Prior Constitutional Provisions

The constitution of 1875 and all amendments thereto except as hereinafter provided shall be superseded by this constitution.

Section 2. Effect On Existing Laws

All laws in force at the time of the adoption of this constitution and consistent therewith shall remain in full force and effect until amended or repealed by the general assembly. All laws inconsistent with this constitution, unless sooner repealed or amended to conform with this constitution, shall remain in full force and effect until July 1, 1946.

Section 3. Effect On Existing Terms of Office

The terms of all persons holding public office to which they have been elected or appointed at the time this constitution shall take effect shall not be vacated or otherwise affected thereby. Section 4. Effect on certain existing courts.—All courts of common pleas now existing, the St. Louis courts of criminal correction, and all circuit court circuits as now established, shall continue until changed or abolished by law. The justices of the peace shall continue to hold their offices and receive the emoluments thereof until their terms of office expire, upon which their records shall be transferred to the magistrate courts.

Section 5. Effect On Existing Rights, Claims

All rights, claims, causes of action and obligations existing and all contracts, prosecutions, recognizances and other instruments executed or entered into and all indictments which shall have been found and informations which shall have been filed and all actions which shall have been instituted and all fines, taxes, penalties and forfeitures assessed, levied, due or owing prior to the adoption of this constitution shall continue to be as valid as if this constitution had not been adopted.

Section 6. Reimbursement for Expenses of Constitutional Election

The general assembly shall appropriate out of the general revenue fund of the state a sum sufficient to reimburse the various counties for the sums legally and properly paid by them to the judges and clerks of the special election called for the purpose of adopting or rejecting this constitution.

ARTICLE XIII: PUBLIC EMPLOYEES

Section 1. Medical Benefits May be Authorized for State Officers, Employees and Their Dependents

Other provisions of this constitution to the contrary notwithstanding, the general assembly may provide or contract for health insurance benefits, including but not limited to hospital, chiropractic, surgical, medical, optical, and dental benefits, for officers and employees of the state and their dependents, including those employees of entities controlled by boards or commissions created by this constitution.

Section 2. Medical Benefits May be Authorized for Political Subdivision Officers, Employees and Their Dependents

Other provisions of this constitution to the contrary notwithstanding, the general assembly may authorize any county, city or other political corporation or subdivision to provide or contract for health insurance benefits, including but not limited to hospital, chiropractic, surgical, medical, optical, and dental benefits, for officers and employees and their dependents.

Section 3. Compensation of State Elected Officials, General Assembly Members and Judges to be Set by Missouri Citizens' Commission On Compensation—Members Qualifications, Terms, Removal, Vacancies, Duties—Procedure

1. Other provisions of this constitution to the contrary notwithstanding, in order to ensure that the power to control the rate of compensation of elected officials of this state is retained and exercised by the tax paying citizens of the state, after the effective date of this section no elected state official, member of the general assembly, or judge, except municipal judges, shall receive compensation for the performance of their duties other than in the amount established for each office by the Missouri citizens' commission on compensation for elected officials established pursuant to the provisions of this section. The term "compensation" includes the salary rate established by law, milage allowances, per diem expense allowances.

2. There is created a commission to be known as the "Missouri Citizens' Commission on Compensation for Elected Officials". The Commission shall be selected in the following manner:

(1) One member of the commission shall be selected at random by the secretary of state from each congressional district from among those registered voters eligible to vote at the time of selection. The secretary of state shall establish policies and procedures for conducting the selection at random. in making the selections, the secretary of state shall establish a selection system to ensure that no more than five of the members shall be from the same political party. The policies shall include, but not be limited to, the method of notifying persons selected and for providing for a new selection if any person declines appointment to the commission;

(2) One member shall be a retired judge appointed by the judges of the supreme court, en banc;

(3) Twelve members shall be appointed by the governor, by and with the advice and consent of the senate. Not more than six of the appointees shall be members of the same political party. of the persons appointed by the governor, one shall be a person who has had experience in the field of personnel management, one shall be a person who is representative of organized labor, one shall be a person representing small business in this state, one shall be the chief executive officer of a business doing an average gross annual business in excess of one million dollars, one shall be a person representing the health care industry, one shall be a person representing agriculture, two shall be persons over the age of sixty years, four shall be citizens of a county of the third classification, two of such citizens selected from a county of the third classification shall be selected from north of the Missouri River and two shall be selected from south of the Missouri River. No two persons selected to represent a county of the third classification shall be from the same county nor shall such persons be appointed from any county represented by an appointment to the commission by the secretary of state pursuant to subdivision (1) of this subsection. 3. All members of the commission shall be residents and registered voters of the state of Missouri. Except as otherwise specifically provided in this section, no state official, no member of the general assembly, no active judge of any court, no employee of the state or any of its institutions, boards, commissions, agencies or other entities, no elected or appointed official or employee of any political subdivision of the state, and no lobbyist as defined by law shall serve as a member of the commission. No immediate family member of any person ineligible for service on the commission under the provisions of this subsection may serve on the commission. The phrase "immediate family" means the parents, spouse, siblings, children, or dependent relative of the person whether or not living in the same household.

4. Members of the commission shall hold office for a term of four years. No person may be appointed to the commission more than once. No member of the commission may be removed from office during the term for which appointed except for incapacity, incompetence, neglect of duty, malfeasance in office, or for a disqualifying change of residence. Any action for removal shall be brought by the attorney general at the request of the governor and shall be heard in the circuit court for the county in which the accused commission member resides.

5. The first appointments to the commission shall be made not later than February 1, 1996, and not later than February first every four years thereafter. All appointments shall be filed with the secretary of state, who shall call the first meeting of the commission not later than March 1, 1996, and shall preside at the first meeting until the commission is organized. The members of the commission shall organize and elect a chairperson and such other officers as the commission finds necessary.

6. Upon a vacancy on the commission, a successor shall be selected and appointed to fill the unexpired term in the same manner as the original appointment was made. The appointment to fill a vacancy shall be made within thirty days of the date the position becomes vacant.

7. Members of the commission shall receive no compensation for their services but shall be reimbursed for their actual and necessary expenses incurred in the performance of their duties from appropriations made for that purpose.

8. The commission shall, beginning in 1996, and every two years thereafter, review and study the relationship of compensation to the duties of all elected state officials, all members of the general assembly, and all judges, except municipal judges, and shall fix the compensation for each respective position. The commission shall file its initial schedule of compensation with the secretary of state and the revisor of statutes no later than the first day of December, 1996, and by the first day of December each two years thereafter. The schedule of compensation shall become effective unless disapproved by concurrent resolution adopted by a two-thirds majority vote the general assembly before February 1 of the year following the filing of the schedule. Each schedule shall be published by the secretary of state as a part of the session laws of the general assembly and may also be published as a separate publication at the discretion of the secretary of state. The schedule shall also be published by the revisor of statutes as a part of the revised statutes of Missouri. The schedule shall apply and represent the compensation for each affected person beginning on the first day of July following the filing of the schedule. in addition to any compensation established by the schedule, the general assembly may provide by appropriation for periodic uniform general cost-of-living increases or decreases for all employees of the state of Missouri and such cost-of-living increases or decreases may also be extended to those persons affected by the compensation schedule fixed by the commission. No cost-of-living increase or decrease granted to any person affected by the schedule shall exceed the uniform general increase or decrease provided for all other state employees by the general assembly.

9. Prior to the filing of any compensation schedule, the commission shall hold no less than four public hearings on such schedule, at different geographical locations within the state, within the four months immediately preceding the filing of the schedule. All meetings, actions, hearings, and business of the commission shall be open to the public, and all records of the commission shall be available for public inspection.

10. Until the first day of July next after the filing of the first schedule by the commission, compensation of the persons affected by this section shall be that in effect on the effective date of this amendment.

11. Schedules filed by the commission shall be subject to referendum upon petition of the voters of this state in the same manner and under the same conditions as a bill enacted by the general assembly.

12. Beginning January 1, 2007, any public official subject to this provision who is convicted in any court of a felony which occurred while in office or who has been removed from office for misconduct or following impeachment shall be disqualified from receiving any pension from the state of Missouri.

13. No compensation schedule filed by the commission after the effective date of this subsection shall take effect for members of the general assembly until January 1, 2009.

www.ingramcontent.com/pod-product-compliance
Lightning Source LLC
Chambersburg PA
CBHW052244220526
45471CB00001B/187